'Under The Cedar'

The Lushingtons of Pyports
A Victorian Family in Cobham
- and elsewhere in Surrey.

Angela
Best wishes
David Taylor

David Taylor

Grosvenor House
Publishing Limited

This book is published by
Grosvenor House Publishing Ltd
28-30 High Street, Guildford, Surrey, GU1 3EL.
www.grosvenorhousepublishing.co.uk

A CIP record for this book
is available from the British Library

ISBN 978-1-78148-403-6

'The hottest day of all. We just managed to get so far as under the cedar - & remained there the rest of the day.'

Susan Lushington
13 August 1893

Pyports from the meadow, 1891.

On the far left is the barn which the Lushingtons used for concerts and dances. In the distance in the tower and spire of St. Andrew's church. On the far right is the cedar under which so many happy hours were spent.

Contents

Illustrations

Foreword by Julian Fellowes

The Lushingtons of Pyports may not quite outrank the Crawleys of Downton Abbey, but in many ways their lives ran in parallel, reflecting the events of the closing years of the nineteenth and the start of the twentieth century as Europe headed for the 'war to end all wars.' When it came, the conflict of 1914-18 would change forever a way of life that had been embedded in English society for many generations.

My interest in the Lushingtons is more than a passing one. My wife descends from Vernon Lushington's first cousin, Fanny Lushington, wife of the man who would succeed his more famous brother as the second Earl Kitchener of Khartoum. These two were Emma's great-grandparents, and so she has a blood link to this fascinating family.

The Lushington archive, which miraculously survived the ravages of time and which was so nearly lost for salvage in World War Two, has now been catalogued by David Taylor. It provides tantalising and rare glimpses into a world that has gone forever. Of course, like the Crawleys of Downton, the Lushingtons had a London home but much of their time was spent in the then rural village of Cobham where Pyports offered them a place to relax and escape the formalities of the London season. Like the Crawleys, they also had a special relationship with their servants which lasted beyond their employment. Additionally a deep sense of duty, nurtured by Vernon's Christian Socialism which was expressed in projects such as the London Working Men's College, Toynbee Hall, and the London Positivist group, led them to develop genuine relationships in Cobham with neighbours and friends who might have been considered outside their social circle.

They were also, unlike me, intensely musical. Music filled their lives and their houses. With Hubert Parry as a friend and tutor the Lushington girls became talented musicians in their own right. This aspect of their time at Pyports was wonderfully captured by the Pre-Raphaelite painter, Arthur Hughes, in *The Home Quartet*, reproduced on the book's cover.

This volume provides us with some wonderful intimate glimpses into the life of this remarkable family and brings to life Cobham in the Victorian era both through the letters and diaries and marvellous photographs from the family album. I hope you find it all as interesting as we do.

Lord Fellowes of West Stafford
July 2015

Introduction and Acknowledgments

In 1982 I wrote the first fully illustrated history of Cobham which was published as *The Book of Cobham*. Subsequently revised and replaced by *Cobham: A History* (2003), the book was a success and went through several printings. As a result I was asked to write a follow up. When researching the first book I was struck by the fact that many of Cobham's well-known past residents had either lived at or had connections with one house in particular: namely Pyports in Church Street. The occupants ranged from the great naval hero Captain Sir William Hoste, who had served under Nelson, to the schoolmaster Samuel Bradnack, whose strong Christian convictions and philanthropic actions gave fresh hope and meaning to the lives of many local people one hundred and sixty years ago.

I decided that my next book should therefore be about Pyports and the people whose lives were linked, not just by the village in which they lived, but also by the old house which they had chosen to make their home. *People of Cobham: The Pyports Connection* was subsequently published in 1985. One disappointment in writing the book was that I felt that I could not do justice to one family in particular – the Lushingtons. Although I gave them two chapters I knew that there was a much bigger story to be told. During the course of my research I submitted a letter to the columns of *Country Life* asking for information about this family. This produced a number of helpful replies and I was eventually given the details of a lady who held the Lushington family archive.

I immediately contacted the archive holder who confirmed that she did indeed hold the family papers which had come to her through her late husband, a lawyer, who had been the executor of Susan Lushington, the last surviving member of the family who died unmarried in 1953. She proceeded to tell me that the archive consisted of many hundreds of letters, photographs and drawings and that some of these directly referred to the family's time at

Pyports. Then began what proved to be a frustrating and fruitless exchange of correspondence and phone calls to make appointments to visit the holder of the archive which were all successively postponed. In the end I was resigned that I would never see the archive and so the book went to press with two rather unsatisfactory chapters based largely on secondary sources.

Over thirty years later I received a telephone call from a man who explained that he was the son of the lady who held the archive. His mother had died and he was in the process of clearing her house. He had found my letters to his mother. Fortunately, although I had moved house, I had retained the same Cobham telephone number and he had been able to track me down. Two days later I collected all the papers which were produced on that visit and which were kindly offered to me.

The archive was lodged for safety at the Surrey History Centre and a basic outline list made of all the papers. I was just then completing my Master's in historical research at Roehampton University and it was suggested by one of one my tutors that I might consider pursuing a doctorate based upon this un-researched archive. Three years later I successfully completed my PhD thesis which I had based on the life of one of the central figures of the Lushington family, namely the lawyer Vernon Lushington, who, in the middle years of the nineteenth century when faced by the challenges of Darwin, and certain German theologians, moved away from his Anglican 'Broad Church' upbringing to become a follower of the French philosopher Auguste Comte whose Positivism and Religion of Humanity offered people a new belief system in which man replaces God. My doctoral thesis created some interest and resulted in a number of published papers and lectures on various aspects of the Lushington family.

The archive is now in the ownership of the Surrey History Centre and with the support of a National Archives Cataloguing Grant I have been able to catalogue all the papers. This task has taken a little over two years. The final catalogue is now on line and available to other researchers. The catalogue is supplemented by eleven photograph albums containing many hitherto unseen views not only of the Lushington family and their friends but also their various houses including Pyports. Although I plan to write a biography of Vernon Lushington, over the years, I have become aware of just how much of the archive relates to local history.

The present book seeks to make up for what my earlier book on Pyports lacked, by reproducing some of these wonderful photographs. For the narrative I have tried to let the family speak for themselves through the hundreds of letters between family members and the especially important diaries of Susan Lushington. Throughout their marriage Vernon and Jane wrote to each other practically every day that they were apart – sometimes more than once. This remarkable and rare exchange of correspondence provides fascinating insights into the couple's family life and their relationship with each other and when put together with the letters and diaries of other family members provides a unique window into life in Cobham at the end of the nineteenth century.

I am grateful to a number of people who have been with me in researching and writing this book. The staff at the Surrey History Centre have been incredibly supportive throughout the project and I am particularly grateful to Mike Page, Julian Pooley, and Robert Simonson who were with me on my journey sorting and cataloguing the Lushington archive. Then there are the many friends I have made as I have delved into the nineteenth century world of the Lushingtons and who have encouraged me in my work and shared ideas and research with me. At Roehampton University there were Peter Edwards, Jenny Hartley and John Tosh. In the USA are Mark Samuels Lasner, Michael Robertson, Margaret Stetz, and Martha Vogeler – all experts in their respective fields. In the United Kingdom I must include Rosemary Ashton, Ian Campbell, the late Anthony Curtis, Henrietta Garnett, Sir John Lushington, Jan Marsh, Fiona MacCarthy, Laura Ponsonby, Gillian Sutherland, and Angela Thirwell. I am very grateful to Ruth Bradbury for her encouragement and help in the production of the book and to Julian Fellowes for kindly providing the Foreword. Finally my thanks go to my wife Carrie for her patience and longsuffering as our lives began, and continue, to be filled with the Lushingtons and their circle. All these have helped in some way. However I take full responsibility for the contents of the book and for any error or omission of fact or attribution that may have occurred. Extracts from letters and diaries in the Lushington archive are reproduced by permission of the Surrey History Centre and, unless otherwise stated, all photographs are from the Lushington albums which are also held at the Centre.

David Taylor
Cobham
October 2015

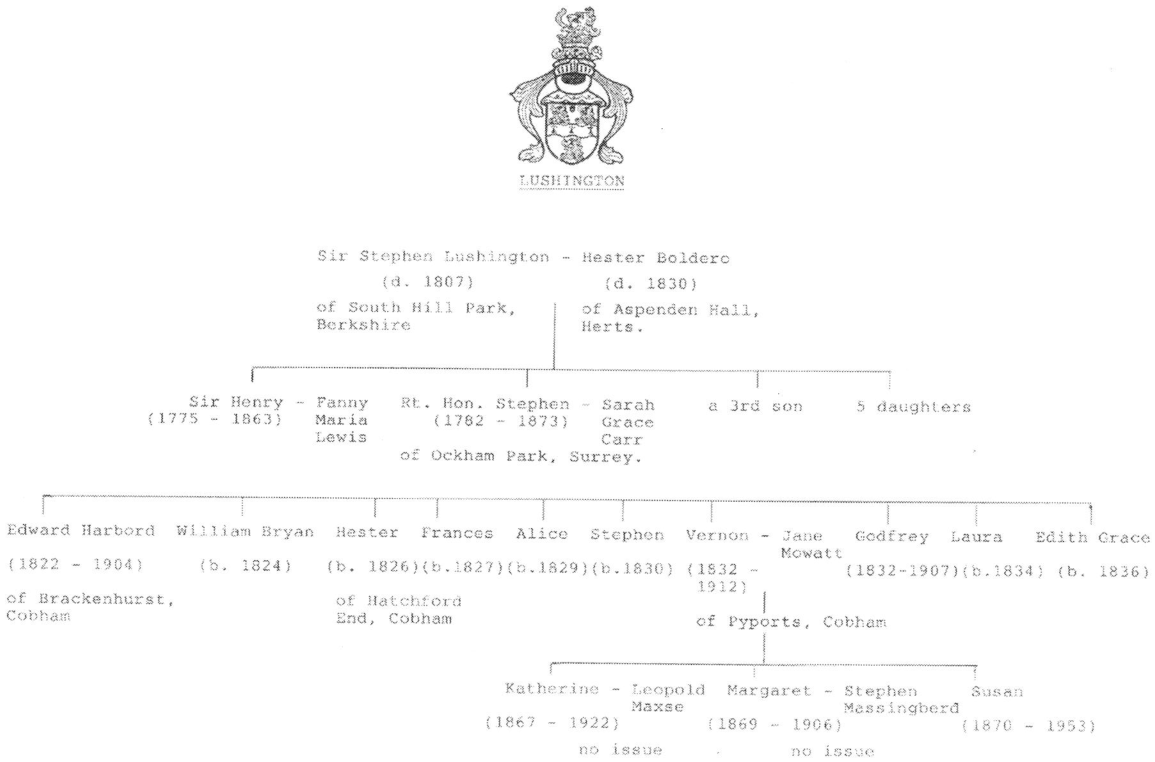

Lushington Family Tree

LOT 16. COLOURED PINK.

COMPRISES

AN ATTRACTIVE

Private Family Residence

Situate immediately opposite the Church,

KNOWN AS

"PYPORTS."

The House which is RED BRICK and TILED, is approached from the road by a flagged way, and is entered by a Roomy Hall.

On the Ground Floor there is DINING-ROOM with BAY WINDOW; EXCELLENT DRAWING-ROOM with BAY Fronting the LAWN Opening into a SMALL TILED CONSERVATORY, Heated with Hot Water; MORNING ROOM and a LARGE PANTRY Fitted with Shelves. On the Right of the Hall is the SERVANTS' WING with a GOOD KITCHEN, SERVANTS' HALL, and FOOTMAN'S ROOM, SCULLERY, and W.C., CAPITAL LARDER and UNDERGROUND CELLARAGE.

On the Upper Floor there are SIX BEDROOMS, TWO DRESSING-ROOMS (Each Large enough for a Bedroom), W.C. At the Top of the Back Staircase is a LARGE LINEN CLOSET and FOUR SERVANTS' ROOMS on the Upper Floor.

In the Pleasure Garden there are some Fine Specimen Cedars, Holly & other Trees.

IN THE YARD ADJOINING THE HOUSE, IS

A BRICK & SLATED DAIRY LINED WITH GLAZED TILES,

AND OPPOSITE IS

A Boarded Knife and Boot-house, and Small Wood Yard near the Scullery, in which is a W.C., and Coal-shed.

In the Stable Yard, which is very Large, is a Brick and Tiled Coach House with Room for Three Carriages, Harness Room, and Man's Bedroom, with Gas laid on. The Stable with Patent Fittings, Contains Four Loose Boxes,

On the opposite side of the Yard is a Large Boarded and Slated Building with 3 Stores, Cow-house and Calf-Pen, another Loose Box, and Storehouse, and also adjoining, a Granary on Iron Pillars, Pigstyes, and Wood-shed. There is also a Large Boarded and Tiled Barn, match-lined throughout inside, in which is an Apple-Room.

AT THE NORTH END OF THE YARD IS A

Brick & Tiled Cottage with 4 Rooms & Washhouse adjoining

THERE IS ALSO UNDERGROUND A LARGE STORE FOR POTATOES.

The Grounds are Tastefully laid out with Summerhouses, &c., together with Productive Park-like Meadow Land, Studded with Fine Old Timber. The whole containing

11a. 3r. 32p. or thereabouts,

Forming a very Enjoyable Residence for a Gentleman of Pleasure and Means. Held together with other Lands on a 21 Years Lease by VERNON LUSHINGTON, ESQ., from Midsummer, 1877.

THE TENANT PAYING ALL RATES AND TAXES AND DOING ALL REPAIRS.

THE APPORTIONED RENT OF THIS LOT BEING

£183 PER ANNUM.

There is a Land Tax of £4 2s. 6d. on this Lot.

Crawter Sale Catalogue 1895.

Pyports – a house with a history

In the shadow of the parish church of St Andrew's Cobham, and only separated from the churchyard by a narrow road, stands Pyports – a large red-brick house which occupies what had historically been one of the most important positions in the village. Its appearance is deceptive. Partially hidden from the road by a high brick wall, the house, at a quick glance, appears to date from the eighteenth century. However, once through the front door, it immediately becomes apparent that it is a great deal older.

A clue to the history of Pyports is in its unusual name, which is probably derived from a family who once lived here. In 1332, when the manor of Cobham belonged to the great Abbey Church of St Peter in Chertsey, the Abbot levied a tax on all the villeins, or villagers, in each of his manors. Schedules were drawn up listing the tenants of each manor and the last name on that for Cobham is William le Pypard, whose surname may mean 'the piper'. The history of the house and its inhabitants can be traced through succeeding centuries with the aid of manorial surveys and title deeds.

In the eighteenth century Pyports passed into the hands of the Skrine and Freeland families and it was probably the latter who transformed the timber-framed house by encasing it in brick. The newly emergent upper middle class families of the Georgian era were immensely proud of their properties and they embellished their homes with walled gardens, gazebos, lawns and shrubberies. They planted new trees in great number and built coach houses and stabling around paved courtyards. For those, like the Freeland family, who could not afford to rebuild their old house, they used the deceit of encasing it in fashionable red brick with smart sliding sash windows. While the interior of the house still retained many of its old features including the wonderful 'queen-post' roof, the exterior now gave the appearance of a compact new house of classical proportions. Further extensions and improvements were made in the early years of the nineteenth century and the house began to take on its present appearance. The prominent bell turret, or cupola, was probably added to the roof at that time, the bell being used to summon the workers from the surrounding farm land.

From the early nineteenth century Pyports was home to a number of interesting and colourful characters whose stories have been told in *People of Cobham: The Pyports Connection.* In 1832 the house was purchased by the Crawters, a family of land agents who came to Cobham from neighbouring Great Bookham in the early years of the nineteenth century.

The Crawters however, never lived in Pyports. Thomas Crawter chose instead to live in a house called Longboyds in Church Street, on a site now occupied by a modern Telephone Exchange. Pyports was part of the Crawter family's investment portfolio and was let to a succession of tenants one of whom was Samuel Wesley Bradnack who came there in about 1857. Bradnack, as his name suggests, was of a prominent Methodist family. His father had been a missionary in the West Indies. Bradnack used Pyports [then known as 'The Cedars'] both as a family home and a place in which to house his school for the sons of Methodist preachers.

One of Bradnack's pupils was Thomas Anstey Guthrie who later became a popular novelist writing under the name of F. Anstey. He is now best remembered for his humorous novel *Vice Versa* which tells the story of a father and son who change bodies with the aid of a magic talisman. As a result the father was made to attend a boarding school to which he had sent his son and which was run by the formidable 'Dr Grimstone'. The book was actually based upon the author's experiences and 'Dr Grimstone' was a caricature of Bradnack. In his autobiography Anstey wrote of how, on meeting his father shortly after the novel was published, Bradnack said, 'I recognised myself in that book.'

By a curious coincidence, in November 1892, Susan Lushington recorded in her diary how she and her Aunt Alice had 'retired to the [Pyports] schoolroom & read out *Vice Versa* straight through – for Aunt Alice to judge whether it would be suitable for Kingsley School. It amused me as it always does.' Anstey's autobiography was not published until 1936 and neither Susan nor her Aunt would have known that what they were reading was based upon actual events that had taken place at Pyports some thirty years earlier.

Such was Bradnack's zeal for the Gospel that he held evangelistic meetings in the barn at Pyports. The Crawters, who had strong links with the parish church across the road (one of them being a churchwarden), were none too happy with these evangelical activities. Eventually Bradnack was pressurised to give up his lease and forced to leave Cobham, taking his school to Surbiton. However he left a lasting legacy in the shape of Cobham's first Methodist Church.

After the Bradnacks came Samuel Lowndes, who spent only a few years there before moving on. Lowndes was followed by George Dines, the much trusted general foreman of Thomas Cubitt, the great builder of the Victorian age who was responsible for the development of large areas of London such as Belgravia, Bloomsbury and Pimlico. The Dines family enjoyed several happy years in Cobham before moving to Surbiton in 1872. The Dines family was followed at Pyports by Stuart Menteth and his family who stayed at the property for five years.

In 1878 Pyports was leased to the lawyer Vernon Lushington, his wife Jane and their three young daughters Katherine ('Kitty'), Margaret and Susan. The Lushingtons were at Pyports for nearly twenty years and what follows is an account of their life in Cobham and the surrounding area drawn from the family's letters and diaries.

The Lushingtons – 'A very perfect household'

The Lushingtons were a family with a long and distinguished history that can be traced back to fourteenth century Kent. On visiting that county in 1905, Vernon Lushington wrote to his daughter, 'Here I am in Kent, as my forefathers were men of Kent. From this place we were digged.'[1] The surname had a variety of spellings including 'Lusington' and 'Lustinton'.

'The Ls are a good race'

Historically members of the Lushington family usually chose either the law or the church as a profession. One who chose the latter was Thomas Lushington (1590-1661). A noted controversial author and theologian, Thomas was born in Sandwich and baptized at Hawkinge. It was said of him that he was, 'Audacious in the pulpit and unconventional out of it.'[2] He was a Socinian, a follower of a religious society that developed around the time of the Reformation who believed that Christ was subordinate to God the father, and 'far from being a substitute for the sins of humanity, Jesus is the bringer of good news and forgiveness, the exemplar of God's love for mankind.'[3] Unconventional religious beliefs continued in the Lushington family. Thomas's theology was not dissimilar to that developed by the Unitarians, or that held by his descendant Vernon Lushington some two hundred years later who became an ardent follower of the French philosopher Auguste Comte. Vernon became a leading member of the London Positivist group and a disciple of Comte's new 'Religion of Humanity' which believed that Christianity and other major faiths had become obsolete.

Vernon Lushington of Pyports could trace his direct ancestry back to Stephen Lushington (1675-1718) of Rodmersham, near Sittingbourne, and Norton Court, near Faversham, Kent. Stephen was a son of Thomas Lushington (1628-1688) who had been made heir of Thomas the Socinian. Stephen married twice and founded the two lines that produced most, if not all, Lushingtons of any note. From the marriage of Stephen Lushington and Catherine Godfrey there descended the Rt. Hon. Stephen Rumbold Lushington (1764-1868) who was a close friend and potential suitor of Jane Austen who wrote to her sister Cassandra:

> I like him very much. I am sure he is clever & a Man of Taste. He got a vol. of Milton last night & spoke of it with Warmth – He is quite an M.P.- very smiling, with an exceeding good address, & readiness of Language – I am rather in love with him – I dare say he is ambitious & Insincere.'

Other descendants in this line included Edmund Law Lushington who married Tennyson's sister Celia, and Franklin Lushington, the friend and executor of Edward Lear.[4]

Following his first wife's death in 1700, Stephen Lushington remarried. His second wife was Jane (nee Petty), the widow of Edmond Fowler of Ash. It was this marriage that produced Henry Lushington (1738-1763) vicar of Eastbourne and his brother Sir Stephen Lushington (1744-1807) of South Hill Park, Berkshire, MP and Chairman of the British East India Company.[5] Sir Stephen married Hester Boldero of Aspenden Hall, Hertfordshire. Whilst their eldest son, Henry (1775-1763) inherited his father's title and married Fanny Maria Lewis, their second son, another Stephen, distinguished himself both in politics and the law. It was this Stephen Lushington who was the father of Vernon Lushington of Pyports. Stephen Lushington was a Broad Churchman and on entering Parliament he pursued the many causes of social and political reform that were his passion including working with William Wilberforce and others to bring about the abolition of the Slave Trade.

The Byron Scandal

In 1816 Stephen Lushington took on one of his most celebrated legal cases – the separation of Lord and Lady Byron. Following advice from two of her distinguished lawyer friends Lady Byron's mother approached Lushington on her daughter's behalf. She later wrote that Lushington was 'the most gentlemanlike, clear headed and clever Man I ever met with' and the counsel and advice he gave led her daughter to remain grateful to him for the rest of her life.

It was almost certainly through Lady Byron that Stephen Lushington met the young woman who became his wife. She was Sarah Grace Carr, the daughter of Thomas William Carr, a Newcastle lawyer who moved to Hampstead in 1807. Carr was a devotee of the arts and knew William Wordsworth and Robert Southey. At Hampstead the Carrs quickly established themselves at the centre of a developing literary coterie which included three pioneering women authors – Joanna Baillie, Anna Barbauld and Maria Edgeworth. Sarah was the eldest of the children born to Carr and his wife. Two of her sisters made particularly good marriages. Isabella Carr married Sir Culling Eardely Smith, a wealthy religious campaigner and founder of the Evangelical Alliance, and Laura married Robert Monsey Rolfe, Baron Cranworth who later became Lord Chancellor. Lady Byron often stayed with the Carr family in Hampstead and when she finally left her husband she went on a tour of the north of England taking Sarah Carr with her as a travelling companion.

'The Mourning Bride'

Stephen Lushington's growing reputation after the Byron affair led to his involvement in an even more celebrated case when he was appointed as one of the legal team to represent Queen Caroline in the matter of her divorce from George IV.[6] In 1821 the Bill of Pains and Penalties was introduced into the House of Lords to deprive the Queen of her title and to dissolve her marriage to the King. The case against the Queen was that she had committed adultery with one of her servants. The Queen's leading counsel was Lord Brougham and Lushington was engaged to act with him as the Queen's civilian adviser. In July of the same year the Queen attempted to attend the coronation but was refused access to Westminster Abbey. Shortly after the coronation, the Queen became ill and died on 8th August. Lushington, as an executor, was with the Queen at her death.

Unfortunately for Lushington and his fiancée, the Queen's death occurred the day before their wedding. In a letter to Henry Brougham, Lushington described how the Queen had sent for him on her death bed, 'My situation was truly painful. You know I was to be married that very morning – Wednesday. I could not, for various reasons, postpone it; so, having taken 2 hours rest, I went to Hampstead was married, and immediately returned to town.'[7] After the Queen's death, Lushington immediately wrote to the Prime Minister, Lord Liverpool, informing him of events and then spent much of the night securing 'all the repositories' at Brandenburg House, the Queen's London home, a task which occupied him until three o'clock the next morning. After two hours sleep, Lushington rushed back to Hampstead to marry Sarah.[8] Immediately after the wedding ceremony Lushington returned to London to meet the Prime Minister who, much to his relief, told him that the Government would defray the expense of the funeral.[9] However the Queen had left instructions that she was to be buried in Brunswick which was her place of birth. It was necessary for Lushington and his new bride to accompany the coffin on its journey and so, what should have been the couple's honeymoon, was spent travelling with the funeral cortege. For this Sarah became known as the 'Mourning Bride'.[10] Joanna Baillie wrote to her friend Lady Dacre, 'We have had a dismal wedding at Mrs Carr's, which I trust will nevertheless prove a happy one. The bride is gone to attend the poor Queen's funeral, with all her bridal bravery laid aside for sable weeds.'[11]

Following their marriage Stephen and Sarah moved to George Street, London where nearly all their nine children were born. None of the children were particularly attractive, which led Maria Edgeworth to comment, 'Mrs Lushington is charming such a real good mother and wife. I wish her children were handsomer.'[12] Sadly Sarah died in 1837 from an aggressive form of cancer. Friends rallied round Stephen and his fellow anti-slavery crusader, Sir Thomas Fowell Buxton, an enthusiastic evangelical Christian, prayed that 'he might be able to console his friend Lushington on the loss of his wife.' Lady Byron's son-in-law, Lord Lovelace, had recently inherited two adjoining estates in Surrey at East Horsley and Ockham. Having chosen to make Horsley Towers his home, Ockham was vacant and at Lady Byron's suggestion it was made available for the man to whom she felt forever indebted.

Ockham Park

Stephen Lushington's open, frank and engaging personality brought him into contact with many well-known people during the middle years of the nineteenth century who were invited to Ockham Park for weekend house parties. These guests included Edward Lear, Elizabeth Gaskell, Benjamin Jowett and John Ruskin. As Stephen's children progressed into their twenties they developed their own circles of friends who also made the journey to Ockham. Among them were the pioneering Christian Socialist F.D. Maurice, William Rossetti, brother of the more famous Pre-Raphaelite artist Dante Gabriel Rossetti, and the sculptor Thomas Woolner, who came to Ockham in the 1850s, to make a medallion of the Judge. Woolner was followed by the artist William Holman Hunt who painted the Judge's portrait in 1862. Lear described the Lushingtons as 'a very perfect household' and a Surrey neighbour of theirs wrote, 'At Ockham Park ... the famous Dr Lushington collected around him the cleverest folk of the day.'[13]

Vernon and Jane Lushington

In 1832 Sarah Lushington gave birth to twin sons at her home in George Street, Westminster. The boys were named Godfrey and Vernon and were so alike that even close friends experienced difficulty in distinguishing them together. Both boys were educated at Cheam School. Godfrey went on to Rugby school and then to Oxford. Vernon went from Cheam to the East India College at Haileybury and then, after a brief spell as a naval cadet, to Trinity College, Cambridge where he distinguished himself as President of the Cambridge Union. He was also elected to the secret debating group known as the Apostles. It was at Cambridge that Vernon first came into contact with the group of Christian Socialists who met at Macmillans' book shop in Trinity Lane. At Cambridge Vernon studied law. He also found time to work for a short spell as an unpaid assistant to Thomas Carlyle.

After graduating Vernon settled into the legal profession working as a barrister on the Northern Circuit where many of his clients were involved in the shipping industry. In 1865 he married Jane, daughter of Francis Mowatt a Liberal MP, who had been born in New South Wales where her father had spent his early career working in the Customs Department in Sydney. In 1831 Mowatt acquired a large estate at Yarralumla on which he built a hunting lodge, bringing out a pack of foxhounds from England to hunt kangaroos and dingoes. The lodge later became Government House, Canberra.

Vernon was keen to share news of his impending marriage with his friends. He wrote to Harry Seeley, 'I must tarry no longer, but tell you my happiness, – that I am engaged to be married. The name of the lady is Miss Jane Mowatt; her father was member for Cambridge some years ago. She is 3 years younger than I am, very tall and very fair, – lovely to see and lovely to know, I think!'[14] When the novelist Elizabeth Gaskell heard from Vernon of the engagement she immediately wrote, 'Your news has given us all great pleasure, for though we never heard of Miss Mowatt before, your account of her charming qualities makes us feel as if you had indeed drawn a prize.'[15]

The couple lived for a short period at Ockham Park under the watchful eye of Vernon's widowed father and his spinster aunt Frances Carr. In 1869 Vernon was appointed Secretary to the Admiralty and with this post came a London home in New Street, Spring Gardens, conveniently close to Whitehall. In 1878 when Vernon left the Admiralty to become a County Court judge he and his family moved to fashionable Kensington Square, number 36, which remained the family's London home until Vernon's death in 1912. At Kensington Square they were surrounded by a number of distinguished residents including celebrated authors, critics, politicians, scientists, scholars and artists, such as the eminent physician Sir John Simon and Richard Buckley Litchfield who was a son-in-law of Charles Darwin and a founder of the Working Men's College. Another family friend, the artist Edward Burne Jones, had lived at No. 41 Kensington Square and, in 1886, the composer Hubert Parry and his family came to live at No. 17.

At their London home the Lushingtons held their weekly 'At Home' to their many friends and other family members on Thursday afternoons. Most weeks they would also host a formal dinner party for their artistic and literary friends, including the aspiring young author, Thomas Hardy.

Vernon and Jane's marriage produced three daughters: Katherine, Margaret and Susan each of whom grew up gifted in the arts – especially in music. Hubert Parry wrote music for them to perform and gave them his new compositions to run through and comment on. Vernon's friend, the artist Arthur Hughes, later painted the wonderful portrait of Jane and her daughters making music at Pyports. Just like his father, Vernon had a very wide circle of friends which included Charles Darwin, Alfred Lord Tennyson, George Eliot, Arthur Sullivan and Hubert Parry.

The Lushington family at Ockham Park c. 1865

From left to right: [under tree] Frances Lushington & Hester Russell (nee Lushington), Ena Russell, Frances Carr, Stephen Lushington, Alice Lushington, Laura Lushington, Godfrey & Beatrice Lushington, Vernon & Jane Lushington.

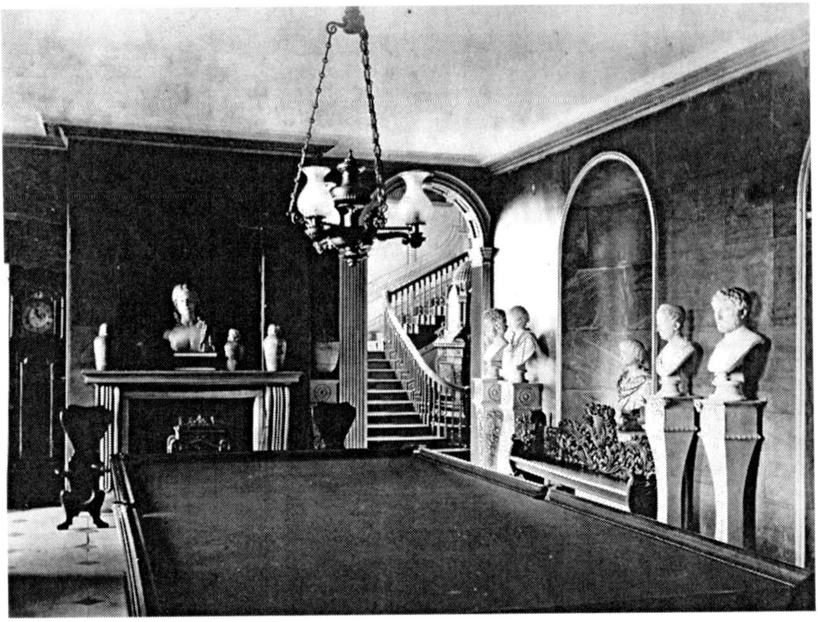

The Entrance Hall and Staircase, Ockham Park, c. 1870.

Dr. Lushington's Study, Ockham Park, c. 1870.

'The Big Drawing Room', Ockham Park, c. 1870.

'The Big Drawing Room', Ockham Park, c. 1870.

Dr Lushington's Panelled Bedroom, Ockham Park, c. 1870.

Miss Carr's Bedroom, Ockham Park, c. 1870.

Frances Carr, Laura Lushington and Stephen Lushington,
Ockham Park, c. 1865.

Vernon, Jane, Kitty, Margaret and Susan Lushington,
Ockham Park, c. 1875

Ockham villagers at Ockham Park c. 1870.
The occasion for this photograph is not known but it may have been for a Lushington family wedding

Miss Laura Lushington's Convalescent Home, Bridge End, Ockham, c. 1870.

Ockham Village School, c. 1870.

Ockham Parish Church, c. 1870. Alice Lushington
and Dr Stephen Lushington.

Wheeler's Farm, Pyrford, 1874.

Vernon Lushington with his daughters at Wheeler's Farm, Pyrford, 1875.

'A word about Pyports'

In addition to a London home, Vernon and Jane Lushington needed a country residence where they could escape not only the formality of London life but also the dreaded yellow smog that descended upon the city in the winter months, sometimes lasting for several days. For a while they lived at Wheeler's Farm, Pyrford, an old house with wonderful views over the water meadows of the river Wey to the ruins of Newark Priory. They were particularly happy here and they are both buried in the graveyard of the little Norman church close by. However a growing family and Vernon's appointment as a Circuit Judge necessitated a larger house in the Home Counties and Pyports in the Surrey village of Cobham was ideally placed.

'a highly favoured spot'

In the second half of the nineteenth century Cobham was still very much a small rural community divided into the old settlements of Church Cobham, Street Cobham and Downside. Church Cobham, where Pyports stands, was centred on the Norman church of St. Andrew. What is now the High Street was then a country lane with only an old farmhouse, a forge and a few cottages fronting it. Church Street was the main street for shopping and here were to be found a stationer's shop, a butcher's, a general store as well as a watchmaker and repairers. Street Cobham had grown up around the busy passing trade on the old London to Portsmouth Road. Here there were several coaching inns, a brewery, a blacksmith and the Post Office. Downside was very much a small rural hamlet with just a few cottages and pub clustered around the village green.

It was about the time the Lushingtons moved to Pyports that an anonymous Cobham resident wrote:

> The air of Cobham is generally considered pure and healthy, many of its inhabitants, as has already been seen, attaining

> a good age. The inhabitants are generally speaking industrious, hardworking people, rather high spirited but easily won by kindness and affability of manner and disposition. They are kind hearted and the old inhabitants some among the gentry were long noted for their kind consideration and charity to the poor: here sickness and distress have ever met with ready and instant relief. It is perhaps to be regretted that strangers complain of want of social feeling among the different classes of society but on the whole I think it is a highly favoured spot and its inhabitants certainly have no reasonable cause to complain but ought to be thankful that so many blessings denied to thousands of our fellow creatures are largely bestowed on us.

It was important that the Lushington's new home should have good access to London. When they first came to Cobham the nearest railway stations were at Esher, Walton-on-Thames and Leatherhead. There had been a number of attempts to bring the railway to Cobham in the middle years of the nineteenth century but all of the proposed schemes took the line close to the royal estate of Claremont at Esher and met with the disapproval of Queen Victoria who had spent many years there as a child. Eventually a new line from London to Guildford via Cobham was agreed and its route was settled between the major landowners. Cobham station was opened in 1885 and proved a great boon to Vernon Lushington and others in Cobham whose work required regular attendance on business in London. The new railway also provided the family with more direct access to their London home and easier access for visitors to Pyports. But even this new line meant that, thanks to Queen Victoria's continuing desire to maintain the privacy of Claremont, Cobham station was well over a mile away from the village centre.

The construction of the new line was watched both with interest and concern by villagers. In September 1883 Charles Combe of Cobham Park, one of the promoters of the new line, wrote to his eldest son, 'The railway is getting on fast: they are nearly at the Bridge over the river, and are burning clay in the field by the water tank.'[15a] The following month Susan Lushington recorded in her diary how she and her Aunt Hester Russell drove in the pony cart to see the new railway being made. She did not record whether they met any of the navvies who were constructing the new line and whose behaviour was causing concern in the neighbourhood. Charles Combe later wrote to his son, 'The railway has nearly got through and we shall be very glad when these fellows finish: the Keeper says they have been a very rough lot this last fortnight.' Combe forbad his daughters to go near the construction work because of the navvies' colourful language.

Negotiating the Lease

Vernon Lushington's busy legal career meant it became Jane's task to seek out a suitable property for the family. In July 1877, after considering a number of houses close to London, Jane wrote to Vernon:

> ... now dearest I am going to say a word about Pyports – I don't know what offer you have made – & perhaps even as I write it is ours – in wh[ich] case I shall of course see no draw backs – but think it & make it delightful but I meant to have spoken to you before about it – had you not been rather impatient with me of suggestions. Don't you think it w[ou]d be wise for us to take it with the option of <u>not</u> continuing the lease at the end of two years so that we may give it a trial & not be bound for an eternal possession – Of course the place has many attractions but I can't help feeling afraid of the soil – the kitchen the churchyard – & other things I need not trouble you with – but of course no amount of prettiness or old fashionedness or picturesqueness w[oul]d make up to us if our children lost their delightful healthiness – & also it is a long way from the station – this of course is for you chiefly to consider – so now I will not say more as I know you do not like me to say any of it.[16]

But Jane's mind was not entirely made up as she explained to her husband a few days later:

> Today I have been to Debenham & Tewson [the letting agents] having gone through every house in their book with trains etc etc & scratched all possible – & I went over the details & saw the photos of nearly all – the Romford one I was thankful to see for I am sure I wouldn't live there. There is a nice one at Cobham w[hi]ch we will go & see – & one at Mill Hill near Hendon w[hic]h looked and sounds very nice if you could be content in that direction.[17]

However Vernon's heart was set on Pyports and he wrote to his wife from Ripley:

> I sallied out on Jackdaw [his horse] this morning at 7 very unwilling to get up but I did. It was a lovely morning, & I rode thru' Bottisdon [Battleston] Hill up the common to Fox Warren, then to Cobham, – where I surveyed Pyports – taking a road you know not of (it, Pyports I mean, looked very pretty), – then home by Pointers & Ockham Common, – to breakfast 'with the family'.[18]

Vernon wrote again the following day:

> Then after tea – we drove to Pyports! On the way we took shelter under a friendly tree from the tail end of a fierce shower (great pleasure this to the children) then at the White Lion or rather Dr Webb's house [Faircroft, Between Streets], we got out, and by a road you know not of [Anvil Lane] circumnavigated Pyports – getting a first rate view of house, garden & park! Very pretty it looked & quite like a home. On our way back by Pointers, we overtook old Watkins. He had just been to the house in obedience to my letter, but found no one in, so was going again tomorrow. He knows the place well, it seems, – having done extensive work there for a former tenant.[19]

'Old Watkins' was John Watkins of Wisley, who styled himself, 'a Clerk of Works & Estate Agent'. He knew the Lushingtons when they were living in Ockham and he had lived earlier at Leigh Hill Cottage, Cobham. His excellent local knowledge proved invaluable to the Lushingtons both in their negations with the landlords and, later, in carrying out improvements and other work at Pyports.

Jane, bowing to her husband's wishes, replied:

> I am afraid my letter of this morning will have seemed rather a trial after your having so entirely taken up your abode at Pyports. – but as I told you before if it is to be ours no one will enjoy it more than I.[20]

Having settled upon Pyports as their country home, the next step was to negotiate both with the existing tenant and the Crawter brothers who proved not the easiest of landlords to deal with. The out-going tenant, Stuart Menteth, wanted the Lushingtons to take possession on the 15th October. 'The date of the new lease has not been precisely fixed between Mr Crawter & me but I presume it is to be the 1 October.'[21] The lease was eventually negotiated to run for twenty one years from Midsummer 1877 but the family did not move in immediately.

On 11 October Jane wrote to her husband that she was proposing to meet Watkins at Pyports a few days later. Watkins warned her that, 'the Crawters are screws & he has had to fight them many times for his clients – so we might as well make up our minds not to count upon much help from them.'[22] Not one to miss an opportunity, Watkins, who could turn his hand to most things including gardening and decorating, offered his services to the Lushingtons for any 'small post' available.

A week later Jane wrote to her husband from Ripley concerning the servants at Pyports:

> It was a gloomy day – but cleared up in the afternoon – so we went off to Pyports from wh[ich] I am just back – I shall hardly have time to tell you all tomorrow. I saw & had some

talk with Whitlock & his very pretty wife. I like both & think them very satisfactory – but they will give us some trouble as I don't think they either of them think much of anything old fashioned – & she evidently thinks Cobham very lonely & far off – & told me everything was very expensive – they have always lived London & in the midst of life – & I sh[oul]d think the floods w[oul]d greatly alarm them! When they come then too there is not a cottage to be heard of – I have told them they can stay for a month – as the Woodwards things can go straight into the house – & they do not want to come before them so by then I hope we shall find something – I am sorry to say a great branch of the cedar is gone – but the place looked very pretty I thought & very improvable with time – the kitchen especially wh[ich] is just covered up with laurels. I had a visit from the 'boy begging' to know if we wd take him on – I said not till we came to live & the gardener had cows to attend to – she [Mrs Whitlock] seemed a nice respectable lady I thought – she told me a good deal of the Menteths – she says that they only lately kept more than 2 servants & did washing at home so they must have been needy people & it is no wonder they spent nothing on the place – she spoke very nicely of them I thought & said Mrs Menteth sold all the milk except what she gave to those who couldn't afford to buy it – & made everything pay – Mrs Arnold took all the butter she could get.[23]

Pyports today is much larger than it was when the Lushingtons took on the lease. The property was considerably enlarged at the end of the end of the nineteenth century after it was purchased by Frank Cripps who employed local architect Leonard Martin to remodel the interior and build a new extension. The old house which the Lushingtons knew was described in 1895 as 'An Attractive Private Family Residence' with a Dining Room with bay window, a Drawing Room, a small Conservatory, a Morning Room and a large Pantry. The servants' wing consisted of a Servants' Hall, Footman's Room, Scullery, WC, larder and underground Cellarage. Upstairs there were six Bedrooms,

Two Dressing Rooms, a WC, a large Linen Closet and four Servants' Rooms. In the yard there was 'A Brick & Slated Dairy lined with glazed tiles' together with a 'Knife and Boot-house'. In the Stable Yard could be found a 'Brick and Tiled Coach House with room for Three Carriages, Harness Room, and Man's Bedroom, with Gas laid on. The Stable with Patent Fittings, Contains Four Loose Boxes.' Elsewhere there were various other buildings including a 'Cow-house and Calf-Pen, loose boxes, storehouses, a Granary, Pigstyes, Wood-shed ... Large Boarded and Tiled Barn Barn ... in which is an Apple-Room.' [24]

The grounds at Pyports were described as being 'Tastefully laid out with Summerhouses, &c., together with Productive Park-like Meadow Land, Studded with Fine Old Timber.' The whole estate contained a little over 11 acres.

Plumbing, Heating and Drains

After signing the lease the maintenance of the house now fell to the Lushingtons. Jane wrote to her husband that Watkins:

> ... advises you not doing up the house thoroughly now – as he says it is stipulated in the lease that it is to be done in 79 – and if we do it now according to the covenant w[hic]h means only 2 coats of paint – even tho' the Crawters might agree to its being done now instead of then – it will not last 14 years – whereas some of the house is quite good enough to go on with now for another few years. Of course this does not apply to the papering w[hic]h will last us as long we like & w[hi]ch like the whitewashing must be done – but to the principal painting – hall, stairs, drawing shutters, doors & etc – w[hic]h have already lasted 14 years untouched & will have to be done some time but are quite passable now.[25]

Equally as important as the internal decorations were the sanitary arrangements and, in December 1879, Jane reported to her husband that she had received a long letter from Watkins about 'W.Cs. & drains.'

> Horlock seems to me the main offender – as it is certainly his place to empty the men servants' affairs – & I can't believe that Willis or William can ever have been told or explained to about its being an E.C. [earth closet] or things could never be in such a state.[26]

'Horlock', who looked after the livestock at Pyports, was a difficult man to deal with as Jane explained to her husband:

> I am afraid I am not so delighted with old Horlock – he seems to me to shirk work so much – & really do but little in the end – well I suppose we must learn our experience with burnt fingers like other people but I feel I wish I lived in a cottage & did my own work myself.[27]

Heating the house was another problem. Vernon wrote to his wife in November 1878, 'This house is undeniably cold, but I hope you won't be miserable.' It was to take a year before the heating problem was tackled as Jane explained:

> Lee came to see me last night about the stove in the Harness Room – & was very sensible as usual ... [he] suggests our having a stove in the Hall – to heat the house throughout & by having the flue carried under the pantry floor & a grating – we sh[oul]d never want a fire in the pantry & the hall would be the warmest room in the house. Someday we must have this done.[28]

'Lee' was probably George Lee who lived in what is now Church Gate House and who, in the 1871 census, was described as a Blacksmith and Carrier. In 1878 Jane wrote, 'hearing that Lee (Carrier) was in the yard & wishing to speak to him of his book I have had him talking to me ever since – I like him & can't help trusting him.'[29] Margaret Lushington wrote some years later, 'I think Lee is a very good gardener & a nice man when he doesn't trample over me.'

Another issue facing the Lushingtons at Pyports was the lack of accommodation for their servants. In particular they wished to find somewhere appropriate for the Woodwards who were to be their faithful servants for many years. In November 1879 Jane wrote to Vernon:

> I was not well & hadn't much sleep for my poor little brain turned over & over the Woodwards cottage question but however I have thought out the only solution to the difficulty that I can think of is this – that you sh[ou]ld go or write ... to Crawter to say we must have a cottage & that we will undertake to build a cottage in the church field – as near the gates as possible & to spend 300£ upon it – if he will remit 12£ of our rent each year ... This w[oul]d of course be a very good thing for him – & as we have to pay 4/- a week for Horlock's cottage – 10£ a year – we sh[ou]ld be receiving 7 1/2 per cent w[hic]h would be good for us too – & into that cottage I would put the Woodwards – as long as they stay there – it would equally close for her dairy work – & not I the garden – w[hic]h was one great grievance to Wickens – who said no gardener would stand his garden being free to other people & to be overlooked from that potato cellar & the cottage windows all day long ... of course the new cottage must be close to the gate for the sake of the dairy.

The House Beautiful

Once the terms of the lease had been negotiated, the sanitation sorted out and the servants' accommodation arranged, the Lushingtons turned to decorating and furnishing Pyports. Jane was concerned about the rising cost of this exercise and anxiously wrote to her husband, 'alas beds & bedding mount up dreadfully but –as you say it must be looked upon as "investment" for beds we must have – & chairs & wash stands!'[30]

When it came to decorating the interior of Pyports, the Lushingtons turned to Morris, Marshall, Faulkner & Co. which Vernon's old friend William Morris had started with a group of friends in 1861 to provide beautiful, hand-crafted products and furnishings for the home. This was highly controversial at the time as it denounced the 'progress' of the machine age by rejecting unnecessary mechanical intervention. Morris's maxim 'Have nothing in your houses that you do not know to be useful or believe to be beautiful' appears to have been followed by the Lushingtons and photographs of the interior of Pyports in the 1880s and 1890s show an extensive use of Morris wallpapers. After some re-decoration of the hall in 1893 Susan Lushington wrote in her diary, 'The red tulip paper & white paint in the hall are simply lovely & how I adore the whole house & garden.' Morris had designed a wild tulip paper in 1884 and a garden tulip paper in 1885. A photograph of the Dining Room shows the walls papered with Morris's 'Willow' design and the dining table appears to be that commissioned by Lushington from Morris's partner Philip Webb in 1864. The School Room was papered with Morris's 'Daisy' pattern – one of his earliest designs from 1864.

'Quiet country life'

The family's 'London Engagement' diary for 1889 closes with the words, 'At this point the Lushingtons retire into quiet country LIFE.' Whilst the Lushingtons appreciated the convenience of fashionable Kensington Square as their London residence, it was always a relief for the family to decamp to Surrey where the first few days would be spent in unpacking and attending to practical matters. The house had to be made 'home' which meant arranging the placement of furniture which had been brought down from London and hanging pictures in all the rooms. Although it was the servant's job to carry out these tasks, they required overseeing by a member of the family. On one such occasion Susan Lushington complained, 'Oh dear how slowly it goes, when you come to all the books – all the china – music – & worst of all – odds and ends.'[31]

On another occasion Susan wrote, 'We arrived just in time for dinner (having taken 2 hours & 40 minutes over it [the journey] – which I think is fairly good as we hardly hurried at all).'

Jane's arrival at Pyports in 1881 with her daughters was described in a letter she wrote to her husband:

> ... for here with <u>every</u> window open & awnings down & everything refreshing to look at – it has been wonderful. We drove down last night & greatly enjoyed it – & the children have been a joy to see & hear happier than happy & full of the beauty of everything – The place looks lovely & the flowers are wonderfully bright. Indeed I never saw the place so pretty – tho' parched up – & Wickens has done nothing but water all day all is well save one disaster – & that is the cow! I am afraid old Nichols has entirely taken you in – Wickens says she is a mongrel & he only hopes you will send her back to sell her where she came from for no one about here would give you sixpence for her. I haven't seen her but even the Woodwards say she is a horribly ugly brute – & she has not given a drop of milk yet & Wickens declares that if you look at her teats you can see she never could – however you can see it has been a trial to him – for he went himself for expecting a 'nice thing' – & his feelings were much hurt. I have not been out of the house all day – for I have been sitting down doing up the schoolroom with wh[ich]. the children are enchanted & say it is far prettier than they ever expected – dear Sue is practising her fiddle – Kit trimming up the pinks in the garden & Peg gone out to get her cello – We shall all be looking for you eagerly tomorrow.

The Lushington girls' pleasure at arriving at Pyports was increased by some relaxation in their studies. London had a tight regime of people visiting to tutor the girls in various subjects, one of them being George Gissing who later became a well-known novelist. One tutor who did come down to Cobham was Miss Tochtermann their German governess. Vernon wrote to Jane:

> Your three children are well & happy, Dearest, as any in the County, Liberal or Conservative. They have roved over

> the garden, visited the calves & the pony, reviewed all their possessions, had a capital tea (2 eggs each) & now they are in the school room ... The garden here was shining in the sun, & Wickens of course at work.[32]

The pleasure and relief of escaping to Pyports from their London home never seemed to diminish over the years as Susan Lushington recorded in her diary in 1893:

> Oh how nice to wake up in one's own room down here. It seems funnily short since we were last here when so much has happened in the meantime – but I do love being here. Of course we unpacked the whole blessed morning till the bell rang ... After tea we walked up & down the beloved broad path with the dogs.

Just as arriving at Pyports was always such a pleasure, leaving brought sadness. On one occasion, after a very short visit to Pyports, Susan wrote, 'I sat up last night – on my windowsill – listening to the nightingales! It was absolutely still – with a faint moon & they sang ... & I could have stayed up all night – but thought it wrong & got into bed at last at 12.15.'[33] When preparing to return to London the Lushington sisters usually went the rounds to say goodbye to their Cobham friends and would spend a day or two packing what was needed to be taken back to London. In 1893 Susan wrote:

> ... the whole day went by making lists & putting out things to be packed ... I wrote to Father and then wandered about in the garden in the twilight saying goodbye to it all – and listening to 'Oh God our Help in Ages past' which came across from the Church in great wafts ... The night was perfect – with the moon just rising behind the Church. I can't say how much I mind going tomorrow – I feel torn up by the roots – & I hate feeling I am leaving this quiet happy time behind me. It has been extraordinarily nice.[34]

The Garden

One of the great delights of Pyports was its setting. After their cramped walled garden in Kensington Square, the Lushingtons' Cobham home offered both a formal pleasure garden and a field in which they could indulge their passion for equestrian pursuits. Lord Nelson's protégé, Admiral Sir William Hoste had spent his last years at Pyports. On returning there in 1828, after a period of absence, it was reported that, 'The sight of the flower garden which he had cultivated with his own hands and laboured incessantly to adorn in every part, appeared to bring only sadness or recollection, deprived, as he now was, of taking any part in his former occupations or even overlooking what before he had so greatly enjoyed.' Sadly Hoste left Cobham shortly after this event for London where he died.

The garden was, and remains, divided into two parts by a ditch or ha-ha. This used to separate the formal garden from the wild meadow which is now given over to horticultural purposes. Parallel to the ha-ha is a broad path which the Lushingtons named 'the quarter deck' – a reference back to Vernon's time as a navy cadet and his period as Secretary to the Admiralty. This was a place to stroll and take daily exercise. The large cedar tree which graces the lawn at Pyports provided a shady place where the family could relax in the summer months either by themselves or with friends. Here tea was taken, letters written and novels read. During one particularly hot spell in 1893 Susan Lushington wrote, 'Just the hottest day that ever was. We lived entirely under the cedar.'[35] A few days later, in the quiet stillness of one summer evening under the cedar, Susan wrote, 'It was so hot you could scarcely breathe – & the singing sounded so clear from the Church.'[36]

Unfortunately the cedar could also present problems. Jane had referred to a branch having fallen shortly before they took up residence and, nearly a year later, the same thing occurred causing Margaret Lushington to write to her mother:

> Such a dredful (sic) thing happened last night we herd (sic) a dreadful crash and we looked out and saw a great branch

of the Ceder (sic) had fallen down but when (we) went and looked at it this morning 3 branches were broken is that not a pitty (sic). We got one fir comb (sic) that was nearly white but I have given it to Lily [probably a servant] because Fraulein says that we shall be able to get a lot more but she cannot.[37]

William Robinson

For advice on their garden the Lushingtons turned to their friend William Robinson, the pioneering gardener. Robinson's ideas on wild gardening spurred the movement that evolved into the English cottage garden, a parallel to the search for honest simplicity and vernacular style of the British Arts and Crafts movement. He is credited as an early practitioner of the mixed herbaceous border of hardy perennial plants. Robinson also championed the 'wild garden', which vanquished the high Victorian pattern garden of planted-out bedding schemes. His new approach to gardening gained popularity through his magazines and books. It was Robinson who later helped Gertrude Jekyll launch her 'career' in gardening.

Vernon Lushington first met Robinson at the Working Men's College in London in the 1860s and later helped him finance the publication of his most influential book, *The English Flower Garden*. Robinson later wrote, 'It was a kindly act at the time, as I was poor, & not many friends, to help me, & so my little ship was launched, & did very well.'[38] The two became firm friends with Lushington often visiting Robinson's home at Gravetye Manor, Sussex and Robinson visiting Pyports. In appreciation of Lushington's help Robinson dedicated his book *The Parks and Gardens of Paris* to him.

In November 1878 Vernon reported to his wife, 'The little gardener is busy as ever: he has got part of the turf down. Nearly all the new fence is up. I think it will look pretty.'[39] Jane's letters often refer to what she called the 'baby garden' – a small area of flower garden, also known as the Little Garden, in the south east corner of Pyports, in the bend of the road.

> The Baby Garden is perfectly lovely – The cherry coloured poppies are a sight to see – & everything seems at its best just now – The sweet peas are as full as ever they were & even more beautiful & the white Lilies & anemones are all ablaze.[40]

The lilies were Jane's particular pleasure and she wrote how Wickens had invited the gardener from the Macaulay's who lived at Leigh Hill House – now the site of Leigh Place – to see the garden. The visitor said that he had never seen the like before, 'so Wickens is very pleased.'[41] Each season at Pyports brought its own particular pleasures and, in 1880, Vernon wrote to Jane:

> A few spring things are out, hyacinth, japonica, daffodils &c – but for the most part all is brown & bare or course, – waiting for the Spring & you. I declined giving any order about the rose trees – dwarf & standard, in front of the kitchen windows – said you were coming on Saturday.
>
> Old Woodward & Mrs Woodward greeted us with smiling faces (& she with a clean white apron) ... Wickens speaks well of his new cottage.[42]

Autumn brought pleasures of another kind which Vernon reported to his wife.

> The Garden is ragged & untidy as it is at this time. We have of course autumn. Such beautiful horse chestnuts are falling from the trees – I invited some of the boys from the Village to come in and gather plunder which they did.[43]

In 1882 Jane was having difficulties with Wickens and wrote to her husband:

> I am very sorry about the garden I always feel that the place is a wilderness when we go down – but I think Wickens' great fault is putting off – everything is postponed to a more convenient opportunity so that as Spring comes the Kitchen

> Garden wants all his time – then when the flowers ought to be seen to – the hay is all engrossing & so on.

After Jane's death, the three girls took an interest in the garden and, in 1886, Margaret complained to her sister Kitty, 'Today our garden is really in a disgraceful state we've plenty of flowers but they're all so desperately untidy & the lawn is one heap of weeds. The two men & the boy spend their days weeding the Kitchen garden paths – its too maddening. I shall tell Wickens that we shall expect vegetables once a week up in London all through the winter.'[44]

During one particularly long and hot spell in August 1893, Susan Lushington wrote:

> The garden is more burnt up than anything I ever saw. The lawn is like brown paper & all the flowers & trees are dying for want of water. There was a regular hurricane blowing – & as we sat there clouds of dust were blown all over us – and the dead leaves were chased across the lawn just like autumn. But then came the blessed rain – & we spent the whole afternoon indoors doing music.[45]

The large field or meadow in which animals could be grazed was also a valuable source of fodder for the livestock and the seasonal haymaking was a feature of the Pyports calendar. Margaret Lushington wrote to her sister Kitty:

> Such a lovely day, how I wish you were here – cold – but a lovely sunset sending long slanting shadows across the field, with a few remaining haycocks trying to dry and Ellen in a blue cotton gown taking out tea to the haymakers with their two dogs – with all its memories this place is still peace to me.[46]

The family tried to be self-sufficient in certain areas and kept a certain amount of livestock including a cow to provide fresh milk but, as Jane explained to her husband:

> Horlock is rather triumphant as the cows gave next to no milk last night – & when Mrs Woodward complained he said it was all for want of oil cake – I wonder if he had told them about it – The white calf had a fine expedition this morning cheered on by boys in the village having got out of the field.[47]

On another occasion Jane had to speak with, 'old Horlock who thinks "everything is going on very nicely" & informed me standing (literally) fondling the pig who leaped up & down with affection that she w[oul]d make a fine mother – & that one day this week he was going to take her to see her better half!'[48] Horlock was probably William Horlock who, at the time of the 1881 census was living in Leatherhead and was described as a 'Gardener, Domestic Servant.'

'The floods are out – far & wide'

Although country living provided many advantages and pleasures, there were also hazards. Pyports was, and still is, sometimes threatened by its close proximity to the river Mole which seasonally floods, disrupting travel in and out of the village. Fortunately the original builders of the house chose the site carefully and so, whilst the river often spilled over into the garden, the house was never affected. In August 1871 Jane wrote to her husband from Pyports:

> The storm seems over but the cruel brown boiling river has overrun his banks & the floods are out and deepening rapidly – it is very disheartening & my poppies are like lumps of heavy sponge & much the same color (sic) – where the rain has soaked into them.[49]

In 1879 Jane's niece, Rowena Russell, wrote to her Aunt informing her of extensive flooding in Cobham with the water, quite up to y[ou]r garden ditch!'[50] This ditch was the ha-ha that still separates the formal garden at Pyports from the former meadow area. In 1892, 'Another pouring wet day!' was followed the next day by, 'The floods are out – far & wide – which ever direction you look.'[51] Three years later Susan humorously wrote to Hugh Montgomery, 'As usual, we are being washed away here and can see nothing but water all round. We are thinking of putting up a boat-house & having a small regatta – shall we give it the Leander Club Colours and institute you as captain?'[52] On another occasion Margaret Lushington wrote to her sister Kitty, 'when the flood is over – if we are left – I have given orders for a family ark to be made.'[53]

Cobham High Street c. 1880. This view from the top of River Hill shows Cobham High Street as the Lushingtons would have known it. [Collection of David Taylor].

Church Street, Cobham c. 1900. Looking towards the junction with the High Street at the top of River Hill. On the right are the shops which the Lushington family would have used. In the distance is the Crown public house which was demolished c. 1905. [Collection of David Taylor].

Pyports: The front entrance, c. 1895.

Pyports: A view from the garden showing the tennis court, 1891.

Pyports: The Yard. A photograph taken
by Archibald Montgomery in 1898.

Pyports: The Barn, 1891.

Pyports: The Little Garden, c. 1895.

Pyports: The Little Garden, c. 1895.

Pyports: 'The Quarter Deck', c. 1898.

Pyports: The Summer House 1891.

Pyports: The Drawing Room 1897.

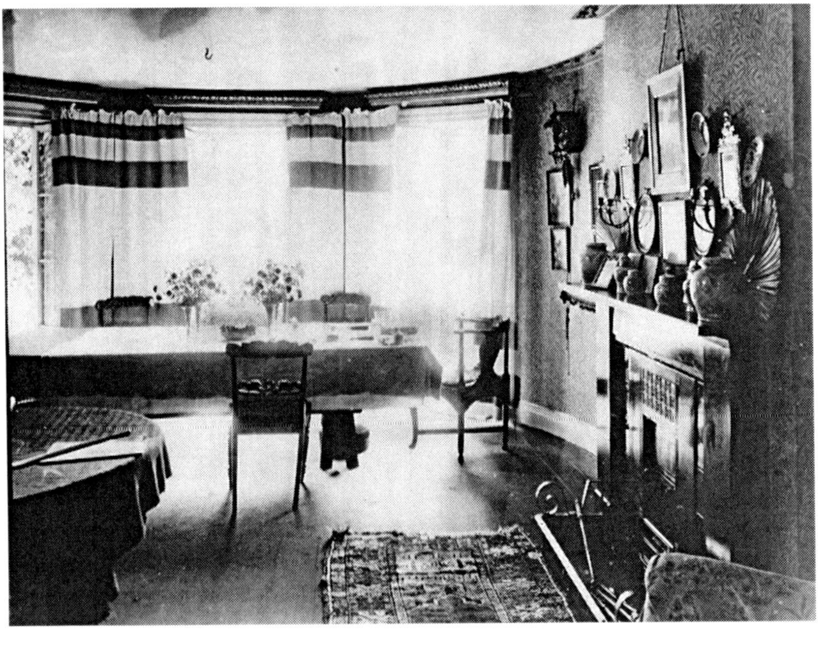

Pyports: The Dining Room 1897.

Pyports: The School Room 1897.
The portrait above the fireplace is probably the lost portrait of Vernon Lushington by Arthur Hughes

Pyports: Vernon Lushington's Room 1897.

Pyports: Susan with Paddy the groom and 'Marble'.

Pyports: Vernon Lushington on 'First Cousin'.

Family and Friends

Vernon was not the only Lushington to live in the Cobham area. Three of his siblings lived close by. Edward Harbord Lushington, Vernon's older brother, together with his wife Mary and their five children had moved from Heathside, Weybridge to Brackenhurst [now Feltonfleet School] in the early 1870s. Edward had served with the Bengal Civil Service between 1842 and 1871 and he and his wife Mary Lushington were regular church attenders at St Andrew's church. They usually called in at Pyports after morning service and sometimes brought visitors with them such as Sir Donald Stewart a senior Indian Army Officer, and Mr & Mrs Seton-Karr who also had connections through India. Edward & Mary's daughter Helen married Francis Reynolds Yonge Radcliffe whose family lived at Ordsall, a large house on Cobham's Fairmile.

One of Vernon's sisters, Hester, married Robert Russell a Captain in the Royal Navy who died just four years after their marriage. The widowed Hester lived for a while at Ripley House, Ripley before moving to Hatchford End, near Ockham with her three children. Her daughter Rowena was particularly close to her Lushington cousins. Susan Lushington recorded how, one day in 1893:

> A[un]t Hester & Cousin Ena came to tea ... & I was so glad they should see the garden when it was nice – & then Fritz [Fritz Bramwell, a family friend] & I played one game of croquet – in which he beat me. After dinner we sat out – but we didn't talk – It was a heavenly night – & we all sat on with our own thoughts.[54]

Laura Lushington, one of Vernon's unmarried sisters, was a regular Pyports visitor. She lived at Bridge End, Ockham with a companion and appears to have been the 'little dumb girl' referred to by Joanna Baillie.[55] A mystery surrounds Laura. There is a curious reference to her in a letter from Jane to Vernon in which she wrote:

> Mr Stedman [the Doctor] thought that Aunt Fanny ought to prepare Laura for the worst & Aunt Fanny had her in her room & spoke solemnly to her – & the poor child has been sobbing all day – & making pathetic efforts to control herself – I fear the idea is gaining ground that she is very ill.[56]

The identity of this illness is a mystery. However in 1878 a legal enquiry was undertaken after which it was declared that Laura was 'a person of unsound mind' and guardians were appointed to look after her affairs.[57] This declaration of Laura as a lunatic appears to have been the Victorian way of dealing with a person who was dumb. Laura made frequent visits overseas for the benefit of her health and wrote to her niece Susan in 1909 of being treated at the Berlin Hospital and then going to Homburg von Huhe 'to have some electric battery treatment three times a week.'[58]

Vernon's older brother William, a friend of Edward Lear, married late in life. His wife was Augusta Godwin-Austen of Shalford House near Guildford and, after their marriage, the couple lived in Bramley. They had a son Philip who was born in 1874. For many years William was Principal Secretary to his uncle, Lord Chancellor Cranworth.

Vernon Lushington's nephew, Hugh Littleton Norris, a talented artist was often at Pyports. He was the son of Archdeacon Norris of Bristol who had married Vernon's sister Edith. Hugh Norris was associated the Newlyn School of Artists in Cornwall. He could be quite difficult at times and Susan complained on one occasion how he was in a 'contradictory mood' when he met their other house guest Olive Maxse. Hugh spent most days at Cobham in sketching and fishing in the river Mole but he did take time out to attend Sunday service at St Andrew's church. On another occasion Hugh was taken from Pyports by his uncle to fish in the lake at Gravetye Manor, the home of Vernon's friend, the gardener William Robinson.

Vernon's two spinster sisters, Alice and Frances, who had worked at the school in Ockham, moved to Kingsley, Hampshire after their father's death where they set up a new school which they named the Ockham Schools. Alice Lushington had earlier been Lady Principal of the first college for Training Women Teachers for Higher Education which later became the Maria Grey Training College.

In July 1893 Susan recorded a rare visit to Pyports from 'Uncle Francis', her mother's brother, Francis Mowatt the liberal MP who worked for a while with Winston Churchill.

Friends

Over the years that the Lushingtons were at Pyports, the place was visited by their friends many of whom were among the 'eminent Victorians' of their day. The following are some of those that are known of through family letters or diaries.

Sir Hubert Parry

In London the composer Sir Hubert Parry [now perhaps best remembered for his stirring musical setting of 'Jerusalem'], his wife Lady Maude and their two daughters Gwen and Dolly were particularly close to the Lushingtons and the two families were forever in and out of each other's houses in Kensington Square. The Lushington girls and their mother first met Parry in 1882 at the home of their mutual friends the Montgomerys at Blessingbourne in Ireland. Jane's letters to her husband were full of Parry's name and how the girls had taken to him and vice versa. Parry delighted in the company of young people, frequently visiting the Lushington girls to try out some new composition of his or play at a concert. Sometimes they were also entrusted to correct proofs for the composer. Parry composed two simple Intermezzi for String Trio dedicated to 'K, M and SL' [Kitty, Margaret and Susan Lushington]. Occasionally members of the Lushington family would travel to the south coast to stay with the Parrys at Rustington. Here they would sail with Parry in his yacht. Kitty was Parry's special favourite and he affectionately named her 'Kittiwake'.

In 1886 Parry brought his family to Pyports for a weekend visit – the event being recorded by Susan Lushington in her diary:

> It was a wet day alas, so we had to have the brougham. I drove to Leatherhead to meet them [the Parrys] & Lady Maude & the children [Dolly and Gwen] drove home with me & Alice on the box but Mr Parry insisted on going in the cart with the luggage. When we got home we all had a nice cosy tea in the schoolroom. Then we sat about in the drawing room till dinner time, Mr Parry playing a little.[59]

The following day Parry gave Dolly a piano lesson whilst Kitty Lushington gave Gwen a violin lesson. When Lady Maude, who was always considered a little delicate, later came down from her room they all went out to inspect the Pyports garden and the barn. In the afternoon the two families went for a drive across Wisley Common to Ripley – the family in the carriage and Hubert Parry on horseback. Parry left the following day leaving Lady Maude and his daughters to stay for a further day.

Occasionally Parry would ride down from London to Cobham. He did this with Susan Lushington one day in 1889 returning the same day by train. The journey took them three hours and they travelled via Richmond Park where they enjoyed jumping the ditches. Parry 'thought the woods & country after Esher quite lovely'. The whole Parry family were at Pyports again later that year enjoying the country air. A good deal of time was given over to riding, walking and making music although one evening the hard working Parry 'retired to his room to work' – presumably on one of his compositions.

Sometimes the Parry girls stayed at Pyports without their parents so that they could take part in one of the concerts given in the Barn such as that given in 1889 when they performed their father's *Tunes for Violin and Piano*.

William Holman Hunt

The artist William Holman Hunt was one of the original members of the Pre-Raphaelite Brotherhood (PRB) and is especially remembered today for his painting *The Light of the World*.

Vernon Lushington first met Hunt and other members of the PRB in the 1850s. It was Vernon who later introduced Edward Burne-Jones to Dante Gabriel Rossetti, an historic meeting which instigated a life-long friendship leading to the second phase of the Pre-Raphaelite movement. Hunt was later invited to visit Ockham Park where he painted the wonderful portrait of Stephen Lushington which now hangs in the National Portrait Gallery's collection at Bodelwyddam Castle in North Wales. Over the years the two families became close friends with Hunt being adopted by the Lushington girls as 'Uncle Holman' and one of Hunt's children being christened Hilary Lushington Hunt.

Susan Lushington recorded in her diary a weekend visit to Pyports by the Hunt family in 1882.[60] The house party that weekend also included the archaeologist and museum director John Henry Middleton, a friend of William Morris who had travelled with him to Iceland when Morris discovered the country's saga literature. Susan recorded that whilst she and 'Aunt Edith' Hunt went to Harvest Festival at St Andrew's on the Sunday, her father with Hunt and Middleton, all men with unconventional religious views, chose to avoid church and go for a walk instead.

Occasionally the Hunt children, like the Parry girls, would stay at Pyports without their parents so that they might benefit from the country air. In 1884 Hunt wrote to Vernon:

> It is a great pleasure to us to have our two children with you and your loving and thoughtful girls – every note from Pyports makes us recognise the delight of the visit the more and enables us to rejoice for the future of good influence which such tender care imparts ... The children have come back very happy brimming over with stories of Pyports friends and looking very much the better for their visit.[61]

In December 1889 Edith Hunt spent a day at Pyports with her daughter Gladys. Susan wrote:

> Oh how I love A[un]t Edie – I think she is one of the most wonderful people in the whole world – & so beautiful – Father loves her – which is so nice & Gladys too is getting

lovely. We had dinner early & then they all went off together by the omnibus.[62]

Arthur Hughes

Another eminent artist of the nineteenth century, Arthur Hughes, was a frequent visitor at Pyports. Although not part of the original Pre-Raphaelite Brotherhood, Hughes was within their wider circle. Vernon first became aware of him when he saw his iconic painting *The Last of England*.[63] He was so impressed by this picture that he immediately wrote to Hughes praising the work.[64] The two eventually met and became life-long friends.

In October 1882 Hughes was at Pyports. He was invited to paint the wonderful portrait of Jane Lushington and her three daughters – *The Home Quartet* [as seen the front cover of this book]. Hughes painted Jane at the piano, with Kitty, Margaret and Susan playing viola, cello and violin. Hughes helped Jane chose the right dress for the painting and, as a personal touch, a bound copy of the score of Beethoven's 'Fidelio' is on the floor by the piano stool. [Vernon and Jane first met at a performance of 'Fidelio'.] Initially Jane was not entirely happy with the painting and she wrote to Vernon:

> It is far too merry – too gaudy I sh[oul]d say – having so many bright coloured things together – the children's dresses are the colour of my poplin & pink sashes & a bright blue cushion behind &c &c &c – otherwise it is lovely ... this morning [I] boldly told him – I must have it made quieter in colour – & he as usual was charming & took it delightfully & after much argument said he thought I was right.[65]

The painting was eventually finished and exhibited in London. In April 1885 Hughes returned to Pyports to work on a now lost portrait of Vernon Lushington.[66] It is possible that it is this painting that can just be seen, above the fireplace, in an old photograph of the school room at Pyports.

Like Parry and the Hunts, Hughes occasionally brought his family to Pyports. In August 1888 they all came for a dance attended by over seventy people. Susan Lushington declared this 'A lovely night ... The Hughes' are darlings.'[67] During the weekend Hughes joined Vernon and the girls riding in the countryside around Cobham. His friendship with the Lushingtons continued into the following century. Hughes often visited Susan after she moved to Hampshire and Margaret at Gunby Hall, Lincolnshire, where his painting of her still hangs.

William Bell Scott

William Bell Scott completed a trio of eminent artists who visited the Lushingtons at Pyports. Scott's best known work today is his decorative scheme for a room at Wallington Hall, Northumberland. He was also a friend of Hunt and Hughes and had close links with the Rossetti family. In 1863 Dante Gabriel Rossetti arranged for the sale of two of Scott's paintings to Vernon. Scott was at Pyports in July 1884 for a short visit. He returned the following year, after Jane's death, and went with Vernon to see her grave at Pyrford church. There he and Vernon had, 'a little talk of the intended monumental stone with its epitaph.'[68]

A year after her husband's visit to Cobham, Scott's wife Letitia made the journey to spend a few days at Pyports. She wrote to A.J. Munby [see pages 58 and 59] of her 'delightful days at Pyports' and, when later acknowledging a Christmas gift of a photograph, she wrote to Susan Lushington, 'The scenery I take to be the garden at Pyports of which I cherish dear remembrances.' Letitia was regarded by her friends as a shrill, neurotic, demanding and difficult person and her marriage was not a happy one. Scott later met Alice Boyd of Penkill Castle, Ayrshire who came to study art in Newcastle and their relationship became very close. Letitia accepted the situation and from the 1860s Scott lived with Alice and Letitia in a ménage à trois in Scotland and London until the end of his life.

Vernon Lushington, like others in Scott's circle, appeared willing to accept his friend's marital situation and was happy to accept invitations for him and Susan to stay at Penkill Castle. During a visit there in 1888 Vernon wrote to his daughter Kitty,

'It is something extraordinary & beautiful too, to see the devoted care Miss Boyd takes of old Mr Scott. It is a kind of friendship I have never seen before.'[69] Later that year it was Alice Boyd who was at Cobham, joining the Lushingtons for tea at Pyports.[70]

Mary De Morgan

The writer Mary De Morgan made at least one visit to Pyports in 1885. Heavily influenced by Hans Christian Andersen, Mary was the author of three volumes of fairy tales. William Morris was fond of her stories and when he was dying in 1896, Mary came to nurse him. Mary's more famous brother was William De Morgan, the most important ceramic artist of the Arts and Crafts Movement and he and his wife Evelyn were also friends of the Lushingtons. In August 1887 Susan and her father went to De Morgan's showroom in Piccadilly to purchase a wedding present for their friend Sybil Buxton of Foxwarren – 'a dish from Father & two little plates from us.' William's father, Augustus De Morgan, was a mathematician and logician who had tutored Byron's daughter Ada.

In her youth, Mary De Morgan earned herself a reputation for tactlessness, apparently at one point telling another artist friend of the Lushingtons, Henry Holiday, 'All artists are fools! Look at yourself and Mr. Solomon!' The wife of the artist Edward Poynter wrote of Mary, 'She chattered awfully, and Louie, she is only just fifteen. I believe a judicious course of snubbing would do her good!' On another occasion she apparently said something to offend the young Bernard Shaw. Mary's tactlessness appears to have been demonstrated when she lunched with the Lushingtons at their London home after which Susan wrote, 'lunch to which Mary De Morgan came – I am really very interested in her – but good heavens she does say rather terrific things!'[71]

Most of Mary's weekend at Cobham was spent in music making with the Lushington girls although time was taken on Sunday to attend a service at St Mary's, Stoke D'Abernon and to visit Jane Lushington's grave at Pyrford.

Sir Leslie Stephen

Sir Leslie Stephen was an author and critic and one of the greatest minds of the Victorian age. He was also the father of Virginia Woolf and Vanessa Bell. His first wife was the daughter of William Makepeace Thackeray. After her death he married Julia Prinsep Jackson, widow of Herbert Duckworth, an old legal friend of Vernon Lushington. Vernon knew Stephen through the Working Men's College, a Christian Socialist enterprise in London where Vernon worked as a volunteer tutor.

Like the Hunts and the Parrys, the Stephen and Lushington families were constantly in and out of each other's London houses. Julia Stephen took a particular maternal interest in the Lushington girls after their mother died and it was she who engineered the marriage of Kitty Lushington to Leopold Maxse, a successful newspaper editor and son of Admiral Maxse of Dunley Hill near Effingham. [A house which Susan Lushington called 'the most unattractive house & place [it] 'dark & Londony – the view dull & the garden quite uninteresting.[72]] The older Duckworth and Stephen girls were particularly close to Kitty and Margaret Lushington and when Julia Stephen died it was Kitty who took the Stephen children under her wing. Members of the Stephen family undoubtedly made many visits to Pyports. However, apart from Kitty's wedding, there is only one other recorded visit. This was made in 1887 when the whole Stephen family came to stay at Pyports whilst the Lushingtons were in London. Margaret Lushington wrote to Kitty how she had been at Cobham supervising, 'the house ... being gradually licked into shape. The whole Stephen family are coming here on Monday.'[73] Shortly after their arrival the grateful Julia Stephen wrote to Vernon:

> It seems to me that fires never burned so brightly and that the house is warmed not only by them. Warm it certainly is – and warmed & refreshed we are already. I do know where the French army meet but the Stephen army has penetrated partout [i.e. everywhere].
>
> Vanessa and Thoby have just come in with glorious cheeks declaring that they have walked a mile. Leslie has

> this moment arrived having walked down [from London] and we are all going to have tea.
>
> Dear Margaret has made the whole house shine with welcome. She thought of everything as her mother would have done.[74]

After returning to London, Julia Stephen and her daughter Stella Duckworth called upon the Lushingtons to inform them that they had left Pyports 'looking lovely – with snowdrops out in the woods.'[75] Vanessa Stephen later married Clive Bell and became a well-known artist within the Bloomsbury Group. It is probably safe to assume that the young Virginia Woolf, only five years old at this time, was also at Pyports at this time with her parents and siblings.

The Stephen family regularly took Talland House in Cornwall during the summer months and it became the fictionalised setting for Virginia Woolf's novel *To The Lighthouse*. In July 1883 the Lushingtons left Pyports for a short visit to Talland House and family letters and diaries tell of their time there. It was on a later visit to Talland House that Leopold Maxse proposed to Kitty in the garden by the jacmanna [the clematis Jackmanii]. Virginia Woolf later described this as her first introduction to 'the passion of love.' The proposal made such an impression on the mind of the young Virginia that it resurfaced thirty five years later in *To The Lighthouse* when she wrote, 'Jacmanna beyond burnt into her eyes ... Jacmanna was bright violet.' As Virginia grew into womanhood she became a close friend of Kitty's although the friendship ceased soon after Virginia and her friends moved to Bloomsbury.

The Litchfields

One of Vernon's oldest and closest friends was Richard Buckley Litchfield who had been with him at Trinity College, Cambridge. Litchfield was a scholar who worked for the Ecclesiastical Commission, managing Church of England property. He was one of the founders of the Working Men's College, where he taught music, mathematics and science in his spare time.

It was the Lushingtons who, in about 1869, introduced Litchfield to Henrietta ("Etty") Darwin, a daughter of Charles Darwin and the two were married in 1871. They came to live just a few doors away from the Lushingtons at 31 Kensington Square. Litchfield's niece by marriage, Gwen Raverat, wrote of her Uncle Richard, 'He was a nice funny little man, whose socks were always coming down; he had an egg-shaped waistcoat, and a fuzzy, waggly, whitey-brown beard, which was quite indistinguishable, both in colour and texture from the Shetland shawl which Aunt Etty generally made him wear round his neck.'[76] Etty Litchfield was a life-long hypochondriac. When she was only 13 years old she developed a cold and a fever, and the doctor recommended that she should have breakfast in bed for a while. Raverat explained that Etty, 'never got up to breakfast again in all her life' and that 'ill health became her profession and absorbing interest.'

Susan Lushington, who dearly loved both the Litchfields, left an amusing description of the couple during their visit to Pyports in 1894. Richard and Etty had come for a weekend and were duly met off the train at Cobham station. The weekend was spent in reading, music making, playing croquet and enjoying the countryside. On one day Susan recorded how they 'all drove over to Ockham [Park]. We wanted to show the Litchfields the garden, as they hadn't been there for 22 years! & we went all over it.'[77] The following day was largely spent in reading aloud to one another and playing croquet between the showers. After this Susan confided to her diary:

> Poor old dear [Richard Litchfield] he interrupted every minute – & asked the most inane questions you ever heard – How extraordinary it is, that a person's intelligence seems to go, with years. One always hopes that would be one thing that would last – and yet, now, a person like Mr Litchfield, who has been in the swing of intellectual people and interests all his life, about the common details of everyday existence seems to be almost as stupid as you can conceive possible – Mr Hills [Jack Hills, widower of

> Stella Duckworth, Virginia's Woolf's half-sister] & I had a discussion and I am always trying to puzzle it out myself, as to how they ever came to marry! Or rather how she ever came to marry him. She must have known everyone – & seen endless people of every sort – & tho' one can't help being extremely fond of him, he is all together the most unmanageable person I ever imagined – One would have thought his hopeless clumsiness, impracticality, & total lack of manners would have offended her almost too rigid sense of minding little things, every minute of the day – and yet here they are – having pulled along together extremely happily for over 20 years.[78]

After the Litchfields left Susan opened her diary again to record her thoughts on Etty.

> Etty also went in the morning. It is so pathetic that constant care of her health seems to have cramped all her interests & energies – and one feels alas – that it must go on getting more so – having no children and no imperative interests or duties of any kind (except nursing her mother which must only be temporary) – It is impossible to talk to a person, who after a few minutes says 'I am afraid there is a slight draught coming against my shoulders' – or 'Perhaps if I talk any more, I might get a headache' You feel that she can never disentangle herself from the thought of her health quite free, for one moment – and it makes it almost impossible to have any real talk with her.[79]

Despite Etty's constant anxieties over her health, for which she took many holidays abroad, and a brush with death when she accidentally swallowed a small quantity of liniment that she had mistaken for medicine, it was Richard who died first in 1903. Etty lived on until 1927, spending the remaining years of her life at Burrow's Hill, Gomshall. She edited a collection of family letters that became a tribute to, and biography of, Emma Darwin who died in 1896. It was also Etty who in 1915, after a questionable evangelist and temperance preacher called Elizabeth Cotton concocted a story about the supposed death bed conversion of Charles Darwin, made a very clear statement that should have ended all such rumours, although even today the story still attracts a certain audience.

Charles Booth

Charles Booth was a Liverpool ship owner and social investigator who in 1886 began, at his own expense, a complete enquiry, street by street and house by house, into the actual economic conditions of the population of London. The results, eventually published in seventeen volumes, as *Life and Labour of the People in London* revealed the appalling and hitherto unrecognised fact that one-third of the population of London were living below the poverty line. Booth's work later led him to make an important contribution to the first Old Age Pensions Act.

As a young man Booth had shared with Vernon Lushington many of the beliefs of radical Liberalism. He became interested in Auguste Comte's Positivism, and, although he felt unable to join in organised Positivism, its philosophy had a lifelong impact on his beliefs. During a visit to the Booths at their Leicestershire home, Gracedieu Manor, Vernon wrote to his daughter Kitty:

> He [Charles Booth] is an optimist. He even goes so far as to call this a most or even the most religious age ... There is nothing like working for others to give one heart & hope; & this he does ... When he goes to Liverpool, or even London ... he always lodges in the East end, – so that he may get to know the people. What food he has, Heaven knows, he seems even here to live like a Hermit on roots & water. He says he loves the Positivists & sometimes calls himself one. I said ... that it was very kind of him. For in truth he must take a wide step before he is really within our camp.[80]

Despite some differing opinions, Booth and Lushington greatly respected each other and had a lifelong friendship into which their respective families were naturally drawn. Booth's wife was descended from Vernon's father's friend the abolitionist Zachary Macaulay, and she became a well-known social reformer and philanthropist in her own right. The Booths made several visits to Pyports, and conversation usually revolved around the social issues of the day. Susan later wrote, 'There is no one in the world like Mrs Booth & I am devoted to them all. Mr Booth was talking most interestingly about the Labour Commission – & he is evidently very satisfied with Georgie's help [George Duckworth was Virginia Woolf's half-brother. He acted as an unpaid secretary to Booth from 1892 to 1902] & says he is so interested & keen. Dodo [the Booth's daughter Antonia] is a little darling too.'[81] On another occasion, after meeting the Booths in London, Susan wrote, 'I don't think I have ever enjoyed my time with Mrs Booth so much before, There is no one like her in the world. I simply love her – & love talking to her. She makes me feel myself more than anyone does.'[82]

A J Munby

A frequent visitor to Pyports was the eccentric Arthur Joseph Munby, a friend of Vernon's from his Cambridge days, and a fellow tutor at the Working Men's College in London. Munby lived for a time at Wheeler's Farm, Pyrford, which was the Lushingtons' home for a short period after their marriage. He was a diarist, poet, barrister and solicitor who developed a fascination with and fetish for, working-class women, particularly those who did hard, dirty, physical labour. He enjoyed nothing more than wandering the streets of London and other industrial cities where he would approach working women and ask them about their lives and the details of their work, while noting their clothes and dialects. These observations went into his journals. Munby's diaries also contain sketches of working women, many of which strongly resemble caricatures of black men: squat, black-faced figures in coats and trousers, with massive feet and hands and protruding lips.

Munby collected hundreds of photographs of female mine workers, kitchen maids, milkmaids, charwomen, acrobats and so on. These diaries and images provide historical information on the lives of working-class Victorian women. In 1854, Munby met Hannah Cullwick, a Shropshire-born maid-of-all-work. They formed a relationship in which Munby was the master and Cullwick the slave, with him training her in the virtues of hard work and loyalty. His scenarios also included elements of age play and infantilism, with Cullwick holding him in her lap or carrying him. The couple secretly married in 1873 but separated in 1877. However Munby continued seeing Hannah until her death in 1909. The marriage remained a secret from all but a few close friends, one of whom was Vernon Lushington and his story has been told in Derek Hudson's fascinating book *Munby – Man of Two Worlds.*

Munby had, in fact, visited Cobham before the Lushingtons moved to Pyports. In 1861 he recorded in his diary how he travelled by train from London to Leatherhead and then walked into Cobham meeting '*by chance*' on the Stoke Road one of the working women who fascinated him. She was Eliza Harris a 'letter carrier' or postwoman. Munby described Cobham at this time as 'thoroughly rural, and picturesque though not antique.' After leaving Cobham Tilt he was impressed by the scene:

> ... where the village road comes down to the Mole and runs besides it. At the junction stands an old-fashioned mill, with a large undershot wheel in full lay, and then comes the mill race, a long quiet strip of water broadening out beyond the weir into a pretty view, with old red houses on one side, and willows on the other, and the church spire in the midst.[83]

The Lushington girls, unaware of Munby's odd marriage, treated him as an eccentric bachelor friend of their father's. He was famous for his unpunctuality which led Susan Lushington to comment, 'Mr Munby to lunch! Very late of course – but so nice & so characteristic.'[84]

Gertrude Bell

In July 1894 a young woman named Gertrude Bell travelled to Cobham to spend the night at Pyports. Gertrude was the granddaughter of the great industrialist Isaac Lowthian Bell, and her family and the Lushingtons were on close terms and were often at each other's 'At Homes' in London. Gertrude later became famous as traveller, writer, political analyst, and administrator in Arabia. Together with T.E Lawrence [Lawrence of Arabia] she is now recognised as almost wholly responsible for creating the Hashamite dynasty and the modern state of Iraq. It was Gertrude who persuaded Winston Churchill to endorse Faisal; the then recently deposed King of Syria, as the first King of Iraq in 1921. Her influence on the new king, led her be described as 'the Uncrowned Queen of Iraq.'

Gertrude was expected to arrive at Cobham station during the evening but she was not on the train. She later appeared at Pyports having got off the train at Claygate by mistake. Susan Lushington took up the event in her diary.

> Father was away for the night, which was unfortunate, but I'm afraid we didn't have a very successful evening. I am so fond of Gertrude – as you know! but she is one of those people who can't help trying to be all things to all men which is fatal. I am so glad that I have seen her at home – for otherwise I should never have known what she was really like ... Poor dear – she is trying to be 'Pyportsy' and ingratiate herself with Margaret by talking music etc. – about which she knows absolutely nothing ... when she & I went out into the garden alone – she was her real self, not putting on anything.[85]

Margaret Lushington commented in her diary, 'Gertrude Bell came for the night – oh dear how insecure one feels she is ... poor girl.' [86] The following morning Gertrude and the younger guests at Pyports decided to discuss, 'the question of women & smoking – to which Gertrude calmly announced that it had ceased to be a question at all – as everyone does it of course – "in fact you two dears, are the only girls I know – who don't."'[87] The next day Margaret wrote to her sister Kitty, 'Gertrude Bell did turn up after all last night but it wasn't a success at all. She posed & posed & we got hot over our argument. Altogether it was a great relief when she went – oh dear.'

Despite their uneasy relationship Susan and Gertrude remained friends for many years. They shared a cabin when, with Gertrude's brother, they travelled together to India for the 1903 Durbar. The Lushington girls also made visits to Gertrude's family home of Red Barns, Redcar from where they would travel over to visit old Sir Lowthian Bell at Roundton Grange, which had been designed for him by the Arts & Crafts architect Philip Webb.

Wilfrid Blunt

The writer and poet Wilfrid Scawen Blunt was married to Lady Anne Noel, daughter of the Earl of Lovelace and granddaughter of Lord Byron. The Blunts spent a good deal of time travelling together through Spain, Algeria, Egypt, the Middle East and India. Lady Anne had a passion for horses and the couple co-founded the Crabbet Arabian Stud. Blunt was a notorious womaniser and his lovers included William Morris's wife Jane. The couple knew the Lushingtons through the Ockham Park connection of the previous generation and, of course, there was a mutual love of horses. In 1891 Susan Lushington received a telegram from Mr. Rendel [of Hatchlands, near Clandon] saying that the, 'Blunts – who were staying with them – proposed coming to lunch with me! What was to be done. I telegraphed back that Father would be away – but I thought couldn't say I wouldn't have them altogether – as they are on a driving tour and this would just be a convenient stop on their way to Weybridge.'[88]

The Blunts duly arrived at Pyports with their daughter Judith. They were keen to see Susan on her horse Hedjay before making a brief call on Mrs Earle at Woodlands on Cobham Fairmile. On their return the Blunts had a tour of the yard and garden at Pyports before lunch. Afterwards coffee was served under the cedar where much of the conversation was about the old days at Ockham Park. Susan talked chiefly with Judith whilst Wilfrid Blunt read the paper. Susan wondered why they had chosen to come knowing that she was alone. However, she considered the visit to have been a success and later wrote:

> Lady Anne kissed me when she went away & seemed really as if she knew me very well! I went out to the yard & watched them drive away. They were really the funniest equipage I ever saw! Two little Arabs leading ... one white & brown speckled – the other chestnut – such sleepy looking little creatures – standing with their heads down & their feet all muddled up together. Then for wheelers – two of the largest, highest, English cart horses you ever saw! ... The harness was of the oldest & most ramshackle description – some of it held together with string – then came the break with Mr Blunt & Judith seated on the box – Lady Anne & a maid inside & a lot of luggage in tin boxes tied round with cord & two grooms in plain clothes, one old man, the other a boy without a collar on! I stood & laughed 'til they had turned the corner.[89]

Mary Ewart

Another old friend of the Lushingtons whose connection stretched back to the previous generation was Mary Anne Ewart the daughter of William Ewart, the Liberal MP who had worked with Stephen Lushington on many of the issues of reform such as the abolition of colonial slavery. Ewart also fought for the abolition of the death penalty and the reform of the established church, as well as promoting educational issues and public libraries. Mary Ewart, a friend of the novelist Elizabeth Gaskell, was an early patron of higher education for women, an interest which she shared with Alice Lushington. Jane Lushington mentions Mary Ewart being at Pyports in August 1879.

The Russell Family

Frequent visitors at Pyports were the children of the Liberal MP Lord Arthur Russell. The Russells had a country home at The Ridgeway, Shere. There were six children and Susan Lushington was particularly close to Flora Russell. After their father's death in 1892, the children were reigned over by their mother, a most formidable lady with all the attributes of Oscar Wilde's 'Lady Bracknell'. Virginia Woolf and Vanessa Bell both considered her a rude tyrannical old woman, with a bloodstained complexion and the manners of a turkey cock.'[90] After visiting the Russells at their house at Shere in 1894, they vowed never to go there again after an encounter with Lady Russell. Susan wrote, 'I simply can't describe to you the coldness of Lady Arthur.' Susan had called at The Ridgeway with a group of friends who had been at the Vaughan Williams' house, High Ashes, near Leith Hill. Most of the group arrived by carriage but two made the journey on horseback and arrived late apologising to her ladyship who 'merely replied – in a chilling voice, "Why, I don't look dismayed – do I."'[91] Lady Russell called at Pyports with her children in 1892. Fortunately she was travelling on to lunch with Mrs Earle at Woodlands and left her children to let their hair down with the Lushingtons.

The Montgomerys of Blessingbourne

Two regular visitors at Pyports were the brothers Hugh 'Hugo' and Archibald 'Archi Montgomery. The Montgomerys were an old Irish family whose family home was a large country house called Blessingbourne, near Five Mile Town, County Tyrone. The boys' father, Hugh de Fellenberg Montgomery, was at Oxford with Hubert Parry and the two remained life-long friends. It is not clear how or when Vernon Lushington first met Montgomery. Hugh junior's God-mother was Lady Byron and so there may have been a connection between the families made in the previous generation. The two families were the closest of friends and the Lushingtons were regular visitors at Blessingbourne which is where they first met Parry. Hugh de Fellenberg Montgomery was a gifted singer and so much of the time during the Lushington family visits was given over to music making and staging concerts in the local village. Family ties between the Montgomerys and the Lushingtons were strengthened when Hugo Montgomery married Mary Massingberd of Gunby Hall, Lincolnshire, sister of Stephen Massingberd who married Margaret Lushington. Archibald Montgomery later married Diana, another of Stephen's sisters. He served in both the Second Boer War and in World War

One and, in 1933, he was appointed Chief of the Imperial Staff. In 1926 Archibald changed his name by Royal Licence to Montgomery Massingberd when his wife inherited Gunby Hall.[91a] Both Hugo and Archi were great horse riders and mounts were always made available to them when they came to Cobham.

In 1893 Susan Lushington recorded, 'It is really rather splendid to have [at Pyports] four members of the Montgomery family! These were the brothers Hugh, Hubert, Walter and Geoffrey. Walter proved to be quite difficult by refusing to come into the dining room to eat breakfast 'or to speak a word to anyone.'[92]

The Howards of Castle Howard

Another family with whom the Lushingtons were on particularly close terms were the Howards of Castle Howard, Yorkshire. Vernon Lushington was an old friend of George Howard, known as the 'Artist Earl', who had a talent for art and moved within the circle of the Pre-Raphaelites and was also a friend of William Morris. It is likely that George Howard knew Vernon Lushington through their links with Trinity College, Cambridge where they had both been students. The Howards lived at Naworth Castle, Cumberland but later took up residence in the great baroque palace of Castle Howard in Yorkshire. They also had a London home designed for them by William Morris's partner, Philip Webb, at No. 1, Palace Green which was within walking distance of the Lushingtons' house in Kensington Square and the families became great friends with the Howards sometimes spending time at Pyports.

On one occasion in August 1893 Susan recorded how, after a long ride over St George's Hill, she and Hubert Howard 'sat down under the cedar and began talking over old Castle Howard days.' They were later joined by Vernon Lushington '& then we got onto religion – & Father – for once – really talked – which we both enjoyed very much. Hubert was interested in hearing about Positivism – and put his side very well – only of course I didn't agree with it – tho' I couldn't say I was wholly with Father either.' [Kitty Lushington had earlier been engaged to Charles Howard for a short period – see Chapter 10.]

Other Visitors to Pyports

In 1893 Susan Lushington recorded how Noel Vaughan Williams rode over to Pyports from High Ashes near Leith Hill bringing with her a young man called Wasey Sterry. Both he and Noel were close friends of Constance Gore Booth the Irish politician, revolutionary, who worked on behalf of the poor and dispossessed and became famous for her leadership role in the Irish Easter Rebellion of 1916 and the subsequent revolutionary struggle for freedom in Ireland. Susan Lushington had met Constance through the Vaughan Williams family and corresponded with her in Ireland. Susan wrote:

> Noel is certainly most amusing – Margaret [Lushington] never realized that Mr Sterry was a Russellite [Charles Taze Russell was an American Christian restorationist minister from Pittsburgh, Pennsylvania and founder of the Bible Student movement from which Jehovah's Witnesses emerged after his death] & was very affable to him! I confess we were rather relived when they refused our invitation to stay to dinner (which Father insisted on!) but I quite enjoyed their visit – & we all watched them off from the yard. Noel on her new invention of a band instead of a saddle.[93]

Others within the Lushington circle of artists, literary and intellectual friends who are known to have made the journey to Pyports were the Positivist John Henry Bridges and A.W. Benn and his wife. Benn was an agnostic and an honorary associate of the Rationalist Press Association. He wrote a number of books on philosophy including *A History of Modern Philosophy*. The Benns were at Pyports in September 1889 and Susan recorded in her diary how, 'At Lunch, she [Mrs Benns] told us all about how she came to be a positivist.' On another occasion Captain The Hon. Norman Grosvenor and his wife stayed for two nights at Pyports. He was a well-known Liberal politician and his wife was a novelist and artist. Their daughter Susan married John Buchan author of *The Thirty Nine Steps* and other novels.

Vernon Lushington 1871.

Jane Lushington with Margaret, Kitty and Susan c. 1880

Susan and Margaret Lushington at Pyports, 1893.
Photograph taken by Evelyn Combe of Cobham Park.

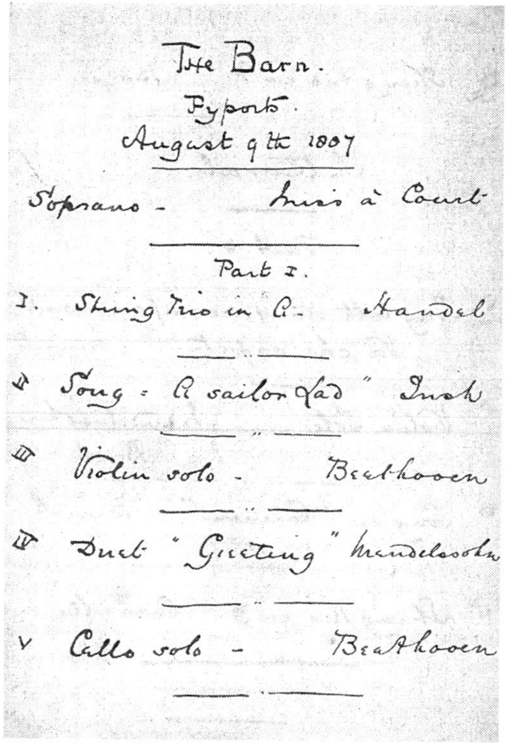

The Barn.
Pyports.
August 9th 1887

Soprano - Miss à Court

Part I.

I. String Trio in C - Handel

II Song: "A sailor lad" Irish

III Violin solo - Beethoven

IV Duet "Greeting" Mendelssohn

V Cello solo - Beethoven

Programme for Concert in the
Pyports Barn 1887

'Quarter Deck, Sunday Morning' Edward
and Margaret Lushington, Easter 1898

Pyports: Susan and Margaret Lushington, Easter 1898

Pyports: Susan Lushington on 'Hedjay' and with 'Leila' her dog, 1891.

Pyports: Susan Lushington with 'Bakshish' and 'Jamnza', 1897

Pyports: Robert the groom with Susan's horse 'Bakshish'.

Samuel Woodward who, with his wife, worked for the Lushingtons at Pyports for many years.

Four visitors to Pyports from the family albums

A.J. Munby

Richard B. Litchfield

Sir Hubert Parry

William Holman Hunt

Hugh Montgomery, Diana Massingberd,
Susan Lushington & Margaret Lushington.
September 1896.

Susan Lushington, Diana Massingberd, Margaret Lushington
& Archibald Montgomery.
October 1894.

Brackenhurst, Cobham, 1899 [now Feltonfleet School].
Home of Edward Lushington.

Edward Harbord Lushington of Brackenhurst, 1897.

'Neighbours – safe or dangerous?'

The Lushingtons soon established themselves among the local community and made new friends in the village but this did not prevent their concerned friend Henrietta 'Etty' Litchfield writing to enquire, 'I'd been wanting to know, but wheresoever is Pyports & what can the Patriarch [Etty's name for her father Charles Darwin] know of y[ou]r neighbours – safe or dangerous?'[94]

Jane Goes Calling

The Lushingtons' circle of friends was enlarged by their new neighbours in Cobham. In the nineteenth century, the etiquette of 'calling' became a firmly established ritual in society, and the calling card an essential part of introductions, invitations and visits. A lady started making calls as soon as she arrived in town to notify everyone that her family had arrived. She usually remained in her carriage while her groom took her card and handed it in. The cards were then placed on a silver salver in the entry hall with the more impressive names displayed on top.

In an undated letter from Pyports to her daughters Jane reported on one such occasion:

> I went out calling! yesterday & happily everyone was doing the same thing so I got through several – Giles first – such a pretty place they have made of it & the house looks too delightful outside – in I did not go – as they were not in – It appears to be all 'Benson' & very pretty Benson too – Then Godleys – out – then Radcliffes – out then Lady Grey – out Mrs Helme – 'going on very well & Baby too' said the smiling happy maid – then Prices – where the fat old white headed butler smiled & bowed as if I were Royalty at least – & said we expect Mrs Price tomorrow & Mr Price next day – then to the Greys – where were all out on the lawn tennising – Ethel & Evelyn Coombe (sic) – Oh how pretty – Blanche Vertue – a very nice sweet looking girl in her white frock &

> the Coombes (sic) seem to 'live for her alone'. I thought her very nice & very bright really – Katie & Norman Radcliffe! – Amy Miss Gallop Jenny & R Cracroft! & one or two others. Mrs Grey was very nice & took me everywhere to see her pretty garden & then I came home & —- Lizzie Cazenove came to dinner – the rest you can imagine. I am going to ask the Hughes for Sunday.[95]

Who were these Cobham families that Jane visited? Jane had started her round on Cobham Fairmile. This was fast becoming a fashionable area to live following the break-up in the 1860s of the Fairmile Farm estate whose fields were being covered by fashionable Victorian villas. One of the first houses to be built here was Sandroyd (now called Benfleet Hall) designed by Phillip Webb for the artist Roddam Spencer Stanhope. Jane's 'Giles' was probably a misspelling of 'Gyles' – the family that then lived at Fairmile Farm – later confusingly known as Fairmile House (there being another Fairmile House on the Portsmouth Road). The 1871 census lists the house as being occupied by Henry James Gyles, a man of independent means. The house which Jane visited was the old house which was replaced by the present Fairmile Court in the early 1880s. Jane's reference to the house as being 'all Benson' might be a reference to the Arts & Crafts designer, William Arthur Smith Benson. Although now best known for his pioneering designs in metal work, Benson had started his career as an architect.

From Fairmile Farm Jane went to the Godleys and the Radcliffes neither of whom were at home. John Alexander Radcliffe, a lawyer, lived at Ordsall, in Fairmile Park Road [later the home of Sir Thomas Sopwith and now called Compton House]. His daughter Helen later married Edward Lushington's son. Jane then called on Lady Barbara Grey at Fairmile House. Lady Grey was the widow of Sir Frederick Grey, the third son of Prime Minister Earl Grey who had introduced the famous Reform Act of 1832 but who is now more remembered for his connection with a blend of tea that carries his name. Jane was indirectly related to the Grey family through her sister Sarah Mowatt who had married Lt. Col. Francis Douglas Grey, a cousin of Sir Frederick. Francis and Sarah's son, Egerton Spencer Grey, later came to live at White House on Cobham Fairmile. After a visit to Lady Grey in 1893 Susan wrote her diary, 'I like her so much – & she is refreshingly un-Cobhamite'[96] – though she does not expand on what being 'Cobhamite' actually involved.

The Helmes were at Fairmile Lea and the Prices lived at Heywood [now the International Community School]. Thomas Price was High Sherriff of Surrey in 1866. From the Price's Jane went to the Greys where she found the whole family out on the lawn playing tennis. Guests there included Ethel and Evelyn Combe of Cobham Park who were to become great friends of the Lushington daughters. 'Lizzie Cazenove' was one of three spinster sisters who lived in Cedar House, Cobham, before later moving to Springfield on Stoke Road.[97] Caroline, Matilda and Elizabeth Cazenove were frequent callers at Pyports and were well known in the village for their good works. A plaque to their memory recording their fifty years in the village can be seen in Cobham church.

Mrs Earle

Another resident on Cobham's Fairmile was Mrs. Theresa Earle, a prolific writer and keen gardener best known for her books in the series *Pot Pouri from a Surrey Garden.* Mrs Earle and her husband moved to Woodlands in about 1879. She described it as, 'a small piece of flat ground surrounding an ordinary suburban house.' Here she created a garden which was greatly admired in her social circle and led to the publication of her best-selling first book. Mrs Earle was the aunt of the wife of the architect Edwin Lutyens and both he and the garden designer Gertrude Jekyll often visited her at Woodlands as did the artist Burne-Jones and the writer Henry James. After visiting Woodlands in 1883 Jane Lushington wrote, 'I must say W. Benson has made a pretty place of it.'[98] Sadly the house was demolished some years ago and has been replaced by another house which has kept the old name.

The Lushingtons often called on Mrs Earle at Woodlands and she, in turn, was a regular visitor at Pyports. On one visit to

Woodlands when she met Nancy Kegan Paul, daughter of the publisher, Susan Lushington wrote, 'Mrs Earle is delightfully warm hearted & generous – but fatally unscrupulous I always feel.'[99] On another occasion at Mrs Earle's Susan met her friend Philip Burne-Jones, artist son of his more famous father.[100] Shortly after the publication of her first book, Mrs Earle's husband Charles was tragically killed in a road accident in 1897. Vernon Lushington met her some months later travelling up to London on the train from Cobham and wrote to Susan:

> I can't tell you how much I admired her grave & bright spirit. She was quite, quite herself, – freely flowing & talking much about him & about herself & her affairs & her new life ... he had made his will with her help – he left her the house at Fairmile with good means to keep it up, but not for other things ... She was also very interesting about her book. I was quite conscious I had never done her justice. Of course her manner is not that which I most love (sweet dignity) – but how affectionate, honest, bright & even brilliant she is, – how good.[101]

Next to Woodlands stands Sandroyd, [now Benfleet Hall]. In 1879 Jane Lushington wrote to her husband that she had been:

> to Mr Wesleys – saw him – tho he was in the agonies of going in to Sanroyd (sic) half packed & all in confusion – he was fascinating as usual but he told Harriett [probably Jane's sister] to her astonishment that he didn't encourage or ever allow much Church going for the boys – or indeed religious education until they were 14 or 15 – & then they left him – so that privately he didn't give much at all. [102]

The Revd. L. H. Wellesley Wesley, a great grandson of Charles Wesley, was vicar of Hatchford and privately home tutored boys including Prince Charles of Saxe-Coburg-Gotha, a grandson of Queen Victoria. When Jane met Wesley he was preparing to move his school into Sandroyd. The school later moved to a new building on the Fairmile which now houses Reeds School.

A leading member of Cobham society at this time was Mary Carrick Moore, niece of Sir John Moore, the great hero of the Peninsular War who died at the Battle of Coruna. In September 1889 Susan called on Miss Moore at her home, Brook Farm on the Stoke Road. 'You feel entirely out of the Cobham atmosphere when you put your foot inside her drive – & when you enter the house – you might be 100 leagues off! She is an old dear & we discussed many things.' On another occasion when Susan called with her sister Margaret they found that Miss Moore was out and, in her absence, the butler was drunk!

In August 1893 Susan met Miss Carrick Moore again at the home of their mutual acquaintance the writer George Meredith who lived at nearby Box Hill.

The 'Funny funny Combes'

Not far from Pyports is Cobham Park, a large baronial hall, designed by Edward Middleton Barry in the style of a French chateau. It was built in the early 1870s and, in the nineteenth century, it was Cobham's 'big house' and home to 'Squire' Charles Combe whose family had made their money in brewing. The Combe children were close in age to the Lushington girls and they quickly made friends. Susan, who always spelt their name 'Coombe', wrote in her diary, 'The Coombes (sic) have quite the funniest manners anyone ever had but I am sure they mean to be nice.' Margaret Lushington called them the 'Funny funny Combes'.

The matriarch of the Combe family was Marianne Combe a figure around whom revolved an atmosphere of mystery. Susan Lushington considered her a difficult person feared by her daughters and, in 1891, Susan wrote in her diary that Evelyn and Ethel Combe had been to tea. 'Poor dears they told us that Mrs Coombe (sic) doesn't allow them to stir out alone – not even in the garden at home – they seemed to speak bitterly & feel it so very much.'[103] Two years later the situation was still much the same when Evelyn and Florence came to tea at Pyports. Susan and Margaret walked back with them to Cobham Park:

> ... talking over all their miseries. It does sound most extraordinary & I think the only possible explanation can be that Mrs Coombe (sic) is mad – for there doesn't seem to be any fixed theory – it is simply all quite un-understandable. Of course one feels if they were different natures something might be done – but then that is just the point being as they are, what can be done. Poor darlings, they were both at least Evelyn very near tears as they told us about it – & it is so dreadful to feel it always goes on, without any hope of its being any different.[104]

In November 1891 Vernon and Susan Lushington were invited to dine at Cobham Park. Susan later wrote, 'It seemed so funny going into that house again. It felt quite like old times – especially as all call me Baby.' The guests included the Rev. Phillips of Stoke Manor House. Susan recorded how:

> Poor Ethel was taken bad in the middle of the dinner – & had to leave the room – but she was alright afterwards. I talked to Evelyn the whole time after dinner – I do really like her so much – somehow it is so nice the way we go on just as if we had never left off seeing each other. I feel I know her quite well, & she me ... Presently when the men came in, Mr Dear joined us – I like him very much & both Mr & Mrs Coombe (sic) were nice & friendly.[105]

The following year the Lushington girls spent New Year's Eve with the Combe children. Part of the day was spent skating on the lake at Cobham Park. Susan Lushington wrote:

> Poor dears – they are simply revelling in being left alone – while Mr & Mrs Coombe (sic) are in India – and they are so happy together ... It is really pathetic how happy they are now that Mr & Mrs Coombe (sic) are gone.

> It [Cobham Park] is turned into a Liberty Hall & everyone does exactly what they like.

The Lushington girls returned to Cobham Park that evening for dinner. Susan wrote how 'Charley Coombe (sic) came forward & said howdedo – quite nicely – but fancy Percy & Harvey both being in smoking coats & trousers!! I think it was quite extraordinary bad manners – don't you? & Harvey Coombe (sic) is so nice.'[106]

The evening seems to have degenerated even more as time went on and the young people began to let their hair down.

> Then we all sang comic songs! It was really funny to see Stephen [Massingberd] standing up to sing the chorus of The Man who broke the bank at Monte Carlo! & even funnier still to see Mildred [Massingberd] dancing lancers with Charley Coombe (sic) rushing round in the grand chain, shouting 'Tarara Boomdeay'. It seemed funnily incongruous to be seeing the New Year in with the Coombes (sic) of all people in the world! But there we were.[107]

The following two days provided further opportunities to skate at Cobham Park and Susan recorded in her diary how they all, 'skated on ... skimming about in the moonlight thinking of many things & times & New Year's Days ... the moon was glorious & threw a shadow the whole time ... and for some reason or other one skated 10 times better than in daylight.'[108] After skating they returned to Pyports for tea after which Susan commented, 'The Coombes (sic) themselves are dears & we bade a sad goodbye for of course when their father & mother are there it is all so different – it is quite likely we may not meet again for years.'[109]

Charles Combe junior's inclination to wild behaviour was demonstrated on another occasion which Margaret Lushington reported to Susan. Margaret had just arrived back in Cobham but 'only just alive for Charlie Coombe (sic) has done his best to run over us at the corner of the village & only Willis's cleverness saved us.'

Susan Lushington has left this account of a dinner party at Cobham Park:

> Margaret & I drove off to dine at the Coombes! (sic) We were only asked at the last moment & were the only guests – the rest was a 'shooting party' of oh such dull & boring people. The only other lady, was Lady Constance Coombe – but she was vulgar to a degree! I went in with Charley Coombe [sic] – who I have always heard was nice – but I couldn't make anything of him. Margaret had a terrible bounder! Mr & Mrs Coombe (sic) themselves were really so kind & nice. I cannot understand about Mrs Coombe (sic) – for whenever I see her – kind is not the word – and so affectionate & easy. We took the fiddles – & played any amount – which I think they all liked – and then Mr Coombe (sic) played to us on his organ. It is the funniest sight I ever saw – to see him gravely playing away – that is to say you work the pedals, & pull out the stops, and the thing winds itself off! He did some bits out of Faust & I joined in on my fiddle and when Margaret began ... he jumped up in a great state of excitement & wanted to rush to the organ that minute – but Mrs Coombe (sic) said 'not now dear' ! and then as soon as we had finished he began. It really didn't sound too bad & it must be the most amusing toy! He told us he played all day long on board the yacht![110]

Later that year Susan recorded in her diary:

> Then the Coombes (sic) appeared [at Pyports] – Evelyn & Gertrude – stayed still 6. They were great dears – but rather melancholy about their affairs generally.[111]

In 1886 Margaret Lushington wrote to Susan, 'The poor Combes have lost their brother Algernon – 10 years old – of brain attack – poor things it was so sudden it must be a great blow to them.'

The Bethells of Emlyn Lodge

Not far from the Combe family were the Bethells who were tenants of the Combe family at Emlyn Lodge, a large Victorian house which stands close to Downside Mill. Charles Bethell and his wife Charlotte Alice moved to Cobham from London in the 1880s. Their son, Wilfred, was about the same age as the Lushington girls and was often at Pyports. However Mrs Bethell was not a welcome visitor as Margaret Lushington explained in a letter to her sister Kitty, 'I do detest Mrs Bethell more than any woman I think I ever saw – she is so vulgar ill-natured & unladylike ... & her ill natured gossip – I felt nearly mad & then I thought they would never go – she stayed 2 whole hours – my wig! & Wilfred stayed till 7.'[112]

The Coape Smiths at Faircroft

In 1882 an excited Susan Lushington wrote, 'Is not it nice that the Coape Smiths are going to take the Webbs House!' The Coape Smiths were an interesting family who were distantly related to the Lushingtons. Vernon Lushington's twin brother Godfrey had married Beatrice Anne Smith whose cousins included Barbara Bodichon, the English educationalist, artist and leading feminist and activist for women's rights; the poet Arthur Hugh Clough; and perhaps the most famous of all – Florence Nightingale.

The Coape Smiths rented Faircroft, a large Victorian house which still stands in Between Streets, set back between Post Boys Row and the access drive to Painshill Park. The house had been built for the local doctor Joseph Webb and was described in the 1890s as, 'an excellently-built Gentleman's Residence in several acres of old-timbered grounds, and highly productive gardens, with stabling for three or four horses.'

Marianne Coape Smith was the widow of Henry Coape Smith, a Major General in the Indian Army, who had died in Australia earlier that year leaving her with five children to raise. These were May, Mona, Ludlow, Ida and Henry who was nicknamed 'Bhaccia' or 'Bhiah'. By all accounts Marianne was a remarkable woman. After her husband's death she brought their children to be educated in England and to pay long visits to their many cousins.

The Coape Smiths and the Lushingtons spent a very happy few weeks together in and out of each other's homes, playing tennis, making music and dancing. Vernon wrote to Jane from Florence where he was on holiday:

> I have today your card, which gives me a glimpse of your bright Sunday, – your walk across the fields with Jim & Mary, & the happiness of dear Mrs Coape-Smith in 'Fair Croft' – I seem to see it all – it must have given great pleasure to you & the children ... I am sure Mrs Coape Smith is happy in your company.[113]

Jane Lushington enlisted Marianne's help when planning a dance in the Pyports barn and she later reported to Vernon:

> The dance was a great success – We had just enough people – 27 – & everyone danced except Ena [Ena Russell] & the eldest Miss Cazenove. Mary Annie [which is how Marianne was known to the Lushingtons] greatly enjoyed it – danced the whole evening principally with her own children & ours – tho everyone wanted to dance with her – The Barn was lovely & really the girls did the supper as well as if Mary had been here – only 8 coats [i.e. men] to 19 girls but no one ever sat out & all danced with great pleasure – we came in to supper at ¼ past one & then when we had gone to bed – the maids went out & had a dance – & there but one opinion – our children looked beautiful in white Baby [Susan Lushington] especially – this morning they have been dancing on the druggett.[114]

Susan Lushington briefly referred this event in her diary, 'gave a delightful dance in eve, all nice people.' The following day she wrote, 'Up very late. Danced in barn with Coape Smiths in morn. Played violin with others ... and went to Coape Smiths for tennis.' Eventually this, like all good things, came to an end.

The Lushingtons were to visit Ireland and the Coape Smiths had to return to London. Marianne wrote to Jane, 'We have all been quite miserable without you ... We are all going to leave Faircroft tomorrow week.' Jane wrote to her husband, 'she [Mrs. Coape Smith] is simply miserable at our going away – & says she shall look back upon these few weeks amongst the brightest & happiest she has had.'

Matthew Arnold of Painshill Cottage

Cobham's most famous resident at this time was Matthew Arnold, one of the greatest minds of nineteenth-century England. Arnold came to live in Cobham in 1873 with his wife and children. They lived at Painshill Cottage which was then part of the Painshill estate which had been purchased by their friend Charles James Leaf. Arnold remained in Cobham until his death fifteen years later. Sadly Painshill Cottage was demolished in the 1960s and is now the site of Matthew Arnold Close. Despite his unorthodox personal religious beliefs, Arnold was a regular attender at St Andrew's church and, while at Cobham, he published some of his most important works including *God and the Bible* and *Last Essays on Church and State*.

It was inevitable that Arnold and both Vernon Lushington and his brother Edward, who lived a short distance from Painshill Cottage, should develop a close friendship despite their differing beliefs in some areas. Close bonds were formed between the two families who were often in and out of each other's houses.

In November 1880 Jane Lushington wrote to her husband from Pyports that, 'Mat Arnold paid me a call to ensure my going [to Painshill Cottage] tonight – he was graver than usual – & gave me a slight account of the big dinner – & found Gladstone's speech "dull".' After further conversation concerning W.E. Forster and Lord Lovelace, Jane enquired about the recent death of the Arnold's pet dachshund 'Geist'.

> ... [Arnold] described Geist's deathbed <u>exactly</u> as if he had been describing his friends – he said it was as 'precisely that of a human' that having lately seen his brother die he was

> struck by the entire similarity 'the struggle for breath then the few last deep breaths & a sigh – & his head fell on the pillow – he was in Mrs Arnold's bed – & then all still. I could hardly realise that it was Geist we had been talking of.[115]

Shortly after this Arnold commemorated the dog in a twenty verse poem – *Geists Grave*. The following are two verses:

> We lay thee, close within our reach,
> Here, where the grass is smooth and warm,
> Between the holly and the beech,
> Where oft we watch'd thy couchant form,
> Asleep, yet lending half an ear
> To travellers on the Portsmouth Road, –
> There build we, O guardian dear,
> Mark'd with a stone, thy last abode.

Arnold's 'dear dogs' were treated like members of the family. Margaret Lushington called on the Arnolds one day to see if Nelly would like to go out for a carriage ride with her, 'but she was just going to have an operation performed on Max [the Arnold's other dachshund] at Cobham Court by the huntsman, with Miss George Smith, Mrs Arnold too fearfully disturbed about it. She said she 'knew they would kill him' & 'I'm much too agitated to talk.'

In November 1882 Arnold wrote to his sister Fanny, 'Then on Saturday I believe William Forster is coming to us and we shall have the Vernon Lushingtons and one or two more people to meet him.'[116] Foster was the Liberal MP who was largely responsible for the pioneering Education Act of 1870.

When Arnold's daughter Lucy married Arnold Whitridge, the son of a New York lawyer, at St Andrew's church in 1884, it was the event of the year. Villagers turned out to wish the couple well and decorated their route to the church with floral arches. Margaret Lushington wrote to her sister Kitty, 'Guy [Lushington] has just told us that Lucy Arnold can't make up her mind what to dress her bridesmaids in & any contributory thoughts will be thankfully received however small, so you ... must set to work &

think & bring back some brilliant ideas.'[117] Lucy and her husband moved to the USA and on one of her return visits to her parents she, with her sister Nelly, called on the Lushingtons at Pyports:

> Lucy & Nelly came to tea last night & were very nice. But Lucy has distinctly an American twang & manner, I'm sorry to say. She wants us very much to go out there & says she will meet us at the landing stage if we will! She has promised to go & see dear Phoebe [a former servant of the Lushingtons who had moved to the USA] & tell her all about us.[118]

In 1887 Arnold wrote to his sister that he and his wife and family had been to a ball at Cobham Park given by Charles Combe. 'I had to go to the ball because Mrs Combe asked me and the girls made me promise I would, but Vernon Lushington took me home before 12, though Combe pursued me into the porch to stop me. But the standing about is dreadful.'[119] Susan Lushington greatly enjoyed the ball; it was her first, and her sisters would not go.

Mrs Arnold looked in on the Lushingtons after church one Sunday in October to try over a tune which she had brought – set to the words of 'Strew on her roses, roses!' Susan wrote 'I dearly love Mrs Arnold – She is so quiet & simple, & so sincere.'[120] Arnold's son, Richard, who was often at Cobham with his parents, quickly made friends both with the Lushington girls and the Combe children. 'Dick' as he was known to his family and friends, was later commemorated by Edward Elgar in one of the famous *Enigma Variations*. On his visits to Pyports, Dick would join the Lushington girls in their music making or go with them to meet the Combe family to skate on the frozen lake at Cobham Park.

The Deacons of Pointers

The Arnolds were close friends of the Deacons of Pointers, Downside. William Deacon was a partner in the banking firm of Williams, Deacon & Co. and on his death the Cobham Parish Magazine carried a fulsome obituary in which it was said 'Cobham [is] bereft of one of its oldest residents and kindest friends.' The Deacon family's philanthropy was particularly to be seen in

Downside where they provided a Working Men's Clubhouse and a new Girl's School. Susan Lushington wrote to her father in an undated letter [but probably written in 1882]:

> On Thursday we all went to the Deacons school-feast, how I loved it and Mrs Deacon! It was such fun swinging the children, and arranging races for them, seeing which comes in first and then procuring those prizes. The Coombes (sic) were there and do you know they are, Ethel and Evelyn, going to Darmstadt into an English Family where they will learn German with a few other children, and Mr [Henry] Holmes is to write and find them the best violin master! On Friday, as you know, it was Kit's birthday and we went for a lovely picnic in Pyrford Woods – some in the carriage and some in the new cart, which has just come home and is lovely ... Eric driving and the new stable boy behind. Molly [the horse] crossed the high lock bridges beautifully, and finally when we went home, they went home by Brackenhurst, and we by the Deacons.

The Buxtons of Foxwarren

Living not far from Cobham was the Buxton family whose home was at Foxwarren which had been built in the middle years of the century on high ground overlooking Wisley Common by Charles Buxton. Buxton's father was Sir Thomas Fowell Buxton MP, the social reformer who had worked with Stephen Lushington and William Wilberforce to bring about the abolition of the slave trade. Susan described a visit to Foxwarren in 1893:

> [We] all went off to tea at Foxwarren – There we found, to our great surprise – a garden party! Consisting of old Mrs Harrison, with Maud & Sid a' Court!! Sir Henry & Lady Roscoe – & then Mrs Hamersly. – The Roscoes amuse me very much ... We strolled about the garden – till dinner – it was the most perfect evening.[121]

'Old Mrs Harrison' was the mother of Fredric Harrison the Positivist whose home was at Sutton Place near Guildford and

Sir Henry Roscoe was a noted research chemist. Margaret Lushington had to leave this event early to collect Adeline Fisher from the railway station. Adeline, who was to stay at Pyports overnight, later married the composer Ralph Vaughan Williams. Adeline and the Lushington girls stayed up late that evening, chatting under the cedar about the Fisher family and 'on all subjects imaginable.' Unfortunately Adeline was of a retiring nature and when, the following day, another guest arrived at Pyports, Susan wrote in her diary, 'I really like her immensely – if only she would be herself when other people are there.' Later that same day more visitors arrived at Pyports including a friend of Vernon's – Mr. Mildred, and Emily 'Pinkie' Ritchie whose brother married a daughter of the novelist William Mackpeace Thackeray. They were to stay for a few days at Pyports. The next day, a Sunday, Miss Ritchie and the Lushington girls played music together before a game of croquet on the lawn at Pyports followed by church.

A few days later Adeline Fisher returned to Pyports with her five brothers and they were later joined by Meg and Harvey Vaughan Williams. On this occasion:

> Adeline produced her camera & took two groups – one included all the dogs ... It was really too funny seeing them all pour in – & stand in a row! We had been rather agitated beforehand as to how it would go off & whether they would any of them talk – but they all seemed so much more cheerful & easy than we expected – it was delightful. I at between the soldier & sailor brother – but conversation was chiefly general. After lunch I had a long talk up & down the lawn, with Herbert Fisher, the Oxford one – all about Oxford, Hubert, Claude Russell, A.L. Smiths & the Murrays etc. He says he feels distinctly that Hubert's set is inferior to himself & it is such a pity that he shouldn't have more distinguished friends.[122]

Herbert Fisher (1865–1940) became an historian, educator, and Liberal politician. He served as President of the Board of Education in David Lloyd George's 1916 to 1922 coalition government.

Some Cobham Characters

The Lushington girls always took time to visit some of the less well-off residents of Cobham and would sometimes call on them with provisions to help in times of need.

The Farrs of Plough Corner Cottage

One such couple were the Farrs who lived in Plough Corner Cottage, just across Downside Bridge from Pyports. The couple kept a general shop at the cottage. In September 1889 Susan 'stopped at old Farr's coming home [from Effingham] & I got out with my violin & played to them – Oh they did enjoy it so – it was simply delightful.'

Later that year, in November, Susan had, 'a long long time with old Farr – He has been in Cobham 51 years – & has seen 5 vicars – he talked a long time about free trade & politics generally – He is really most interesting.' After a further visit to the Farrs a few weeks later, Susan wrote, 'this time we didn't talk of politics or strikes – but of our family – I had no idea that they had known Grandpapa & Ockham so well – I like them both so much.' The following month Susan recorded how the Farrs asked if she would accept one of their photographs. 'They had never been taken all their lives before!'

In December 1892 Susan took her sister Margaret for a Christmas visit to the Farrs:

> We had the most lovely morning imaginable – but it was beginning to get dark when M & I started forth. We went first to Mrs. Farr who was really delightful. She invented a good many stories of Mrs. Coombe (sic) which of course I had to contradict! But she was so cheerful & bright & when I told her it was Kitty's wedding day [i.e. anniversary] she said, 'Ah well – I had 59 & if she is anything like as happy as we were – she'll do well! Mrs. [Farr's husband had died a year or two earlier.]

After an earlier visit that year to Mrs Farr Susan recorded in her diary:

> She [Mrs Farr] is an old heroine – & nobody knows it – but I love & admire her more every time I see her – She told me a long story of her little servant – who had been an endless worry & trouble to her – & finally had ran away!

The following year Susan called to say goodbye to her old friend as the Lushingtons were packing up to leave for London.

> I had such a specially nice time with Mrs Farr – we talked – as usual of her husband – & she said how she had his photograph opposite to her bed – and that as she lay & looked at it – she felt she must talk – & she did – & never a single night passed without her talking to him & thinking of him.[123]

The Chinnerys of Chilbrook Farm

The Lushingtons sometimes combined a visit to the Farrs with one to the Chinnerys who lived at the other end of Plough Lane in Chilbrook Farm. In 1892 Susan recorded in her diary:

> ... I had such a nice time with [Mrs Chinnery]. Poor old dear she seemed very weak & sad & said she was afraid she had got 'indigestion of the lungs'! We walked home in the pitch dark & I had tea & finished up our parcels before dinner. In the evening I sent off my cards & then somehow we were very late – of course Xmas falling on a Sunday turns Friday into Xmas Eve.

Vernon Lushington later recorded a conversation with 'old Chinnery the Farmer'.

> I met him yesterday in Plough Lane, & had a nice word with him. I asked him how he was & then said there was a man who beat us both, named old Ledger who had not

spent 20 shillings on a doctor in 60 years. Well, s[ai]d. old Chinnery – he is an extraordinary man, & in more ways than one. But until I was ill after the blizzard, I don't think I spent £5 on a doctor in all my life. That day I happened to be killing of a pig, & the boy neglected the fire, & I had to see to it, & my face got all hot from the fire, – & then I had to face the blizzard all the way to Wesleys – So I got the Erysipelas [an infection causing the skin to go red] – He said he c[oul]d walk to Wesley's & back now. He had walked to Chapel that morning, & now he was going to have 5 minutes chat with old Farr – Old Chinnery is a darling certainly, & so gentle. I c[oul]d find no fault with him but that he was all in black. I forgot to tell you that in speaking of his health he said. 'But then I've been a moderate man, moderate in everything, a moderate man. Temperance, you know Judge, is the law of health' – The other day I found him going into Cobham Village on Saturday afternoon. Why, I asked [he replied] 'to buy a Methodist paper Mrs Chinnery can't get to Chapel now, so she liked a Methody paper on Sunday afternoon.'

Mrs Hughes of Post Boys Row

Another local character known to the Lushingtons was Julia Hughes who kept a draper's shop in Post Boys Row, Between Streets [now 'Pipe-line Interiors']. Kitty wrote to her sister Margaret saying how she and Susan had:

> walked across the fields with your telegram [to the Post Office at Street Cobham] & coming home we went into old Mrs Hughes' shop to buy some labels – what a dear amusing old creature she is. It appears that "her relatives" were French Hugenots (sic) & in the French revolution – they 'flew' to England 'a mother, five children & a chest of plate. Mrs Hughes still possesses the old French bible & she so enjoys the Cobham library for she gets books about the Hugenots (sic) & the other day she had one which she discovered to be 'by a relative'.

The Village Barber

In need of a haircut one day, Vernon Lushington visited the Cobham barber who told him the curious story of his life and how he had come to Cobham:

> I have had my hair cut in the Village by an ex-Sergeant of the 10th Hussars. He is established round the corner close to Mrs Kippen's the Fishmonger, & is the son of Mr Lewis 'the Minister' who owns some cottages here, Lee's & Levett's etc. [Henry Levett lived in Longboyds Farm in the High Street]. He told me the story of his life, wh[ich] was rather a strange one. As a boy he was apprenticed to a hairdresser in London but his father 'knocked him about' with a stick, which he could not stand, & he ran away from home. He ran first into Somersetshire, eventually he enlisted in the 10th Hussars & worked himself up to be a Sergeant, also cut Officer's hair, went out to Egypt, was in the camel corps, was wounded 'stabbed in the knee' came home. He had never seen his Father or communicated with him since he ran away. He now went home in uniform & presented himself at the door 'What is your business?' s[ai]d his Father. 'I'll tell you, he answered, if you let me in.' His Father said 'Come in' – 'I walked in & going to the Chimney-piece, I pointed to the 2 photographs & s[ai]d 'That's my Father & that's my Mother' – the old man, he said, shed tears of joy: The mother was dead. Then the son bought himself out of the Army, started a hairdresser's shop in Fleet Street, sang on the Stage, sang also in Church on Sundays, 'took the Solo in Jackson's Te Deum' ...... married & now has settled here to be near his Father (who is now off to Matlock for the Water cure) – that was his story. He had cut my hair short enough – I think after the pattern of his Colonel. He has had a good deal of hair cutting experience, & I hope may be useful here. I can't tell you yet whether I really like him, I a little distrust vagabond lives, but he speaks freely & gently He looks the soldier, wears smart moustaches, & if I am not mistaken, thinks well of himself.[124]

The Social Round

Church Going

As was usual in the Victorian era, much of Cobham's social life revolved around the parish church. However this presented some problems for the Lushingtons for although Jane was a regular churchgoer, Vernon, who had been brought up in a family with very liberal religious views, became a devoted follower of Auguste Comte and his 'Religion of Humanity'. For him, although there was nothing wrong with traditional Christianity, it had become a thing of the past and man was now set to replace God in the overall scheme of things. This inevitably brought some pressures to the Lushingtons' marriage but they learned to tolerate each other's beliefs and Jane and her daughters attended church, both St. Andrew's in Cobham and St. Mary's in the adjoining parish of Stoke D'Abernon.

A visit to St. Mary's was recorded in a letter from Margaret to her sister Susan in 1886:

> We had a very tumble down service at Stoke this morning – & the organ had apparently gone for a holiday so we had a harmonium, which the dear little organist played even worse than the organ.[125]

The previous year Susan Lushington had attended a service at St. Mary's and confided in her diary, 'To Stoke church in morn. Much nicer than Cobham.'[126]

St. Andrew's church was more conveniently placed for them as it was just across the road from Pyports. The building underwent a number of 'restorations' and enlargements during the nineteenth century. However these were not to the taste of the Lushingtons. Vernon was a member of the Society for the Protection of Ancient Buildings (or 'Anti-Scrape' as it became popularly known) which had been founded by his friend William Morris in response to the ill-advised and poorly undertaken 'restorations' that were taking place in many of the country's ancient parish churches. In 1887 Susan Lushington visited St Andrew's with her friend Miss Banfield:

> After lunch, Miss Banfield said she would like to see the church, so Margaret & I went over with her. It has been a most beautiful church, but oh dear, it has been restored out of its seven senses. It has the most fearful coloured glass & altogether is ruined. We stayed there a long time – discussing the anti-scrape society when we suddenly discovered a harmonium & Margaret & I made a day of it & played lots of things. The Pastoral Symphony, He Shall feed His Flock & the March in Scipio, then we came back & walked around the garden & visited the stables.[127]

But it was not just the fabric of the building that came in for criticism. The preaching and the music at Cobham were not always to the taste of the Lushingtons. In 1899 Susan Lushington wrote in her diary:

> We had a grand discussion at breakfast about Church & we finally decided to go to Cobham – to hear the new vicar – so Margaret & I & the two boys set off. We sat quiet in the back & it was very funny finding ourselves there again – After all the vicar didn't preach – but the new curate did. I am afraid very feebly – however good preaching & a good man don't always go together – so we will hope for the best. The singing was still very bad – not perhaps so much the hymns – but the chants were terribly flat.[128]

The 'new vicar' was the Reverend Thomas Jervais Edwards, vicar of Cobham from 1889 to 1902. His wife died in the same year that they arrived in Cobham, leading the whole village into mourning and causing the cancellation of festivities such as the Combe family's Christmas Ball.

> Came home exhausted to lunch – to hear the sad news of Mrs Edward's death at Cobham. I am so sorry for the poor

> little daughter. I am sure she is not very happy with the Father – & now of course the Coombes (sic) ball will be put off – which will be very disappointing to lots of people.[129]

It was probably Mrs. Edwards to whom Kitty was referring in an undated letter to Susan:

> I have no interesting news except that the new Vicar's wife is such an invalid that she is only kept alive by a spoonful of milk every hour night & day & that the curate's wife ... is going to have a baby & consequently I don't think either will be of much use anyway for sometime & I'm afraid we haven't gained much by their being married.

Thomas Edwards came in for Susan's stricture after she attended evening service at St. Andrew's in October 1892:

> The singing is certainly improved – & they did the hymns quite beautifully. We had 'Oft in danger – oft in woe' – & then 'Grant us o Lord' – but to a different tune – which I didn't know – but this of course I couldn't like like the old one. I thought it very beautiful. Altogether I enjoyed the service very much – it was so quiet & peaceful – with the exception of the sermon from the vicar – which was odious. The whole moral & doctrine was 'the great hereafter' as if it mattered to no one what happened down here. It was the most exquisite starlight night as we walked home.[130]

The following month it was the Curate who met with Susan's displeasure. 'The Curate preached but I didn't very much care for it.'[131] The curate was the Reverend Wilson. He had dined with the Lushingtons that same month and Susan wrote in her diary, 'I quite liked him only I think he is a little bit commonplace.' It was probably Wilson of whom she had written on an earlier occasion:

> On Friday, the new Curate and his wife came home and Cobham bells pealed forth their utmost for the occasion.

> Wasn't it romantic! Today he preached in Church, and Guy [Lushington] described it as if his voice was between two ruled lines, like a copybook, and he could neither go above or below them![132]

But it was not all bad. On one occasion in 1887 Susan recorded that she 'went off to Cobham Church with Miss Wetton. Strange to say we had a very nice sermon from Mr Young.'

The Harvest Festival

In September 1883 Jane Lushington wrote to her husband in France, 'I have been to Cobham to Church to a grand Harvest thanksgiving service ... it was a pretty sight – the flowers most beautiful & the whole effect of the people all dressed in Sunday best (& almost everyone with a bouquet & a general feeling of festivity) was very pleasant. There was a great deal of music but not of the best.'[133]

The meadow at Pyports was given over to Harvest celebrations and, in September 1878, Jane wrote to her husband explaining at some length how the vicar tried to obtain a merry go round to put up in the meadow for the Harvest celebrations:

> You'll be amazed to hear that she [Kitty Lushington] – & I – are quite in love with Mr Banks!![134] – he has been here this morning – so merry & full of fun – certainly no airs or 'proud priest' about him – he came about the Boiler! – you must know that our servants think him so delightful in the pulpit & on Sunday last week in the evening he promised to continue his sermon on Wednesday evening – so on Wed – I had a petition to do without all but John as they all wished to go to Kirk & off they went – but – no Mr Banks – & great the disappointment – so this morning I abused him & he sent us into fits of laughter – over why he never appeared on Wednesday – his merry go round has failed him – & feeling the disappointment w[oul]d be great to many – he has been doing his best to supply its place – he heard of one at the Crystal Palace – nearer still – a man at Leatherhead – and

one at Barnet fair – so he started at ½ past seven from here in search of the merry go round – 1st Leatherhead – one man engaged at Oxford! But had a brother with one – some way off – he alas engaged to something fair I forget where – then to the Crystal Palace – & they were both already hired for the 10th! – and then on to Barnet fair – such a scene as he described ... how little we knew the exciting lives that these merry go rounds must live – his description was like a bit of Dickens – but he still has a hope from a man who has not yet answered – he told us he didn't go dressed as a clergyman to Barnet fair but 'in plain clothes'.

Then he is a keen tonic sol fa-ist & has had no end of trouble to get anyone to help him or take it up – he was always fond of music but couldn't read & was bemoaning his troubles to an Irish curate who promised to make him read the Elijah for his own pleasure in a 12 month – of course he laughed at him – but determined to try – & tho' he has had to teach himself has done quite enough to give himself immense pleasure – the worst is he cannot get an organist to teach it – & yet he says when he teaches the boys a hymn from the modulator – they learn in a day what the organist takes weeks to drum into them – he says he has had lots of Hullahs[135] men – but he never had one who w[oul]d read.[136]

Of course, the main focus of the Harvest celebrations was the actual church service and Jane wrote to her husband describing the preparations for this:

We mustered a goodly number for the practice [of the harvest anthem] & Mr Banks is a most severe conductor but he did it well & had it over & over again & dear Kit for one greatly enjoyed it & sung away with all her little heart singing alto from the old notation just as easily as from her own book – she is quite in love with Mr Banks – Nelly same down to the service & is going to lunch here today – & Guy has been down with flowers &c for the decorations & 30 flags wh[ich] they have made – old Horlack foremost in

> the choir was a splendid sight with a white waistcoat & his good old face burnished up like brass for the occasion at the top of it ... The field is already full of people putting up tents, mowing the grass where the dancing is to be &c &c &c – & the first person I met when I went to see Horlack was Mr Banks with sleeves tucked up in our yard where he and his men have been putting up the copper just by the side of the Woodwards cottage – against the wall. The dear children come today – & I must meet them & Alice [Lushington] at Weybridge at 2.20 [pm].

The preparations for the Harvest Festival featured again in another letter apparently written the following day to that above:

> All the world is here for the festival tomorrow. I have just come from the Church swarming with ladies & beginning to look very beautiful. E Buxton there ... taking an organ lesson. Our <u>contributions</u> amuse me – a large golden pumpkin a huge vegetable marrow & plenty of <u>fig</u> leaves & ferns – I have just got my dear chicks [the Lushington children] poor Alice [Lushington] she could not keep her tears at parting with them & the children say poor Fanny [Lushington] cried all the morning.

To this letter the young Kitty Lushington added a note of her own:

> I have just been down to the village with Fraulein [the girls' German tutor]. Everybody seems coming to the Harvest Feast. I went to the choir to sing yesterday evening it was too nice there is such a nice Anthem and Te Deum. <u>I</u> didn't go to bed till <u>TEN</u> and yet I slept very well ...There is to be a merry-go-round and I going on it. I must soon finish because I want to go in the field and see Guy put the posts up.

The Flower Show

Whilst Pyports with its large meadow was used for Harvest festivities, other neighbours took turn in holding that other all-important village event: the annual Flower Show. In 1885 Susan Lushington recorded how she, 'went to Cobham Flower Show at the Macaulays. Great fun. Tent for Art & Industry. Most amusing. Everybody there. Band.'[137] The Macaulays lived at Leigh Hill House, a large old house that formerly stood overlooking the river.

The venue for the Flower Show appears to have moved around the village and in 1893 it was held in the grounds of Knowle Park [later the Schiff Home of Recovery and until recently the site of the offices of Cargill International]. Susan wrote about this event in her diary:

> At 4 we drove up to the Earley Cookes to the Cobham Flower Show – but somehow one felt it was quite wrong not having it at the MacCauleys. Being mixed with Miss Burmester's Garden Party, everyone's clothes were so terribly smart & a fearful atmosphere of boredom seemed to pervade everywhere! One talked to all the usual people – Coombes (sic), Charley Patton etc. & we escaped the first minute we could which was by 5.45! The only thing to cheer up one's spirits at all was to gallop Bamboo home & have a large tea with jam sandwiches under the Cedar![138]

John Earley Cooke owned the Oxshott brickfields and had built 'Knowle Hill' on land that was formerly part of the Fairmile Farm estate in 1857. 'Miss Burmester' was his niece.

Dancing at Pyports

Friends and family members were sometimes invited by the Lushingtons to dances in the barn at Pyports. In 1892 Susan Lushington recorded one such occasion in her diary. The barn was decorated with greenery, 'It all looked deliciously bowery – only we hadn't nearly finished when the rain came on & we came in to the lunch.' Unfortunately the rain persisted and the Japanese lanterns, which were to have decorated the garden, were hung instead in the Barn. Guests started to arrive by train in the late afternoon. They included 'Hugo' Montgomery, Mr Mildred, Fritz Bramwell, Margaret Stanley and Hilda Robinson.

> We had had fearful qualms as to our number of men and telegraphed right & left to Mr Balfour, Mr Pollock, Mr Harry Stephens & Hubert [Montgomery] to bring Mr Ponsonby, Mr Du Maurier to bring Mr Newenham etc. etc. but I think that we really had plenty in the end. Mr Clough, who came to breakfast yesterday, suggested several & Mr H.B. Smith did come at his suggestion! But he himself wouldn't come – said he was too frightened!

'Mr Ponsonby' was Arthur Ponsonby son of Sir Henry Ponsonby, Queen Victoria's Private Secretary. Arthur later married Dolly Parry. 'Mr Du Maurier' was Gerald Du Maurier the actor and theatrical manager and uncle of Dame Daphne Du Maurier.

After dinner other guests began to arrive. These included Violet Maxse, Dolly Parry and Philip Burne-Jones. 'Then came the Williams – Roland & Sybil [cousins of Ralph Vaughan Williams] & Sid [Deacon] from Poynters.' The bad weather meant that the garden could not be used as planned and so:

> we all had to sit out in between the dances in the tent – but for so small a dance it didn't really much matter. The music – a pianist & a fiddler – were simply perfect ... Mr Du Maurier – who had been very silent & difficult to get on with when he first arrived – quite cheered up – and I danced with him thrice. However he remained for 8 dances after supper with Violet in the house – which I don't think was very good form! Mr H.B. Smith & Mr [Jack] Hills who both came down by a late train – were charming & Fritz Bramwell is always just so nice as he can be. Altogether our average of dancing was quite extraordinarily good. Archie [Montgomery], Fritz, Hugh [Montgomery], Gerald [Duckworth], Sid [Deacon] & Stephen [Massingberd] are simply perfect ... & then for the girls – it was a real joy to watch Sylvia du Maurier. She dances quite beautifully & is so enchantingly pretty. Then there was dear Die [Diana Massingberd] who looked lovely in black & Mildred &

> Mary [both Massingberds] both looked charming too & Margaret Stanley. Dolly Parry also looked nicer than I have ever seen her & Hilda's dancing is so delightful & graceful. We all went in to supper together – which was much the nicest plan for a small dance & then we had four separate tables. I was alone at mine with Roland Williams, Mr Du Maurier & Violet .... We went out again after supper & kept it up til 3.30! and then back again for soup & strawberries & to bed I don't know when! We watched the Williams drive away in full daylight!

Some of the guests stayed overnight at Pyports and those that could not be accommodated stayed at neighbouring houses such as Church Gate House which was then the home of the Reading family. The guests left during the course of the following morning and. Susan noted, 'We shan't see Sylvia [du Maurier] again until she is married which is rather a fearful thought. I do so wonder whether she and Arthur Davies will be happy.' Then of Gerald Duckworth [Virginia Woolf's half-brother] Susan wrote, 'Poor dear Gerald I have been rather unhappy about him these last few days. He has been so impossible to manage with other people! He is absolutely sensitive and huffy & his manners are simply hopelessly bad – tho I must say, I am very fond of him through it all.'

These remarks about Sylvia Du Maurier's forthcoming marriage are interesting in the light of more recent speculation concerning her friendship with the writer J.M. Barrie. Sylvia married Arthur Llewelyn Davies and the couple had five children, all boys. In 1898 Sylvia met Barrie at a dinner party. The two developed a close friendship and Barrie spent a considerable amount of time at the Davies's home. Sylvia encouraged her boys' friendship with Barrie and they became the inspiration for his stories of Peter Pan. After the death of her husband in 1907, and Barrie's later divorce, the two remained close but did not marry. Sylvia died of cancer in 1910 and Barrie became one of the boys' three guardians and helped provide for them.

Christmas

On Boxing Day 1890 Margaret Lushington wrote to Hugh Montgomery describing Christmas festivities at Pyports:

> If Sue & I were both Archbishops of this village, we couldn't have spent a more Parochial Xmas – carols have never ceased outside the front door (woefully out of tune) festivities for ever in the barn & the Cobham band have just serenaded us & been to lunch & when we feebly said they played nicely – they joyfully encored the whole thing![139]

Susan Lushington's 1892 diary covers the preparations for, and the celebration of, Christmas.

> Thursday 22nd December
> Margaret and I were lazy & didn't come till I don't know when & then there was a lot to do. All the Irish and abroad letters have to be written & sent off today. Meanwhile new stove had been lit – & the hall smelt exactly like a Workhouse Ward – M & I sung Xmas Carols in cracked voices & felt like aged Paupers. I ran out to Mrs Souter's to buy cards.
>
> Friday 23rd December
> M & I were very late for breakfast & then set to as hard as we could. First there were our Indian letters – I always like getting them done first of all. It seemed so strange & horrid to think that Xmas would all be gone & forgotten by the time he got it! Then I wrote to my two dear little Bradford children – while M did up the parcels & so on till lunch.

On Christmas Eve, Susan planned to go to the Christmas Hunt at Ripley but Willis said that 'the ground was too hard to go – but he sent across & found that the hounds were going – so I said I would go too.' Eventually Susan made her way to Ripley, 'but there was no sign of the meet. However at last I came upon the Onslows & we all walked up the village together. The hounds did appear – but I don't think they did much hunting – it was much too hard. Then there were also the Coombes (sic), Harvey, Mr Dear & two friends riding – & all the others in the brake.

The Onslows lived at 'Ripley Court' and were related to the Onslows of Clandon Park. After the hunt started Susan:

> trotted home – but oh the cold. I felt chilled to my heart. I had cocoa when I got in – & M[argaret] & I started on a large box of Charhonel sweets that Gerald had sent. M has really made the house quite lovely – with holly & ivy all round everywhere. I love Xmas decorations & I wish one did it at other times of the year too! The minute after lunch suddenly in walked Aunt Alice & the two children. It really is great fun having them all. We just had two or three more parcels to do up & then it was all done & I couldn't believe it was Xmas Eve & all finished! Kit & Leo came by the 4.8 & Father came down to tea. We music'd in the evening & were very happy although dear Leo seems rather headachy. We sat up talking rather late of course – & gave each other all our presents – which was much nicer than in public!

Susan's diary continues with the following entries for Christmas Day and Boxing Day:

> Xmas Morning
> The most perfect day that could be – bright clear frost & blue sky – It was so refreshing coming down to find those two dear children in a frantic state of excitement over their stockings having been filled! Kitty & Margaret went up last night & did it & had such fun over it. Adele actually hung out Margaret's & Jessie put a cracker in it so by the time I woke up there she was sitting up in bed with a green paper cap on! There was only one drawback to breakfast & that was poor Leo coming down evidently feeling very bad & not inclined for anything or anybody! However Kitty was simply wonderful & made it alright. After breakfast we quickly gave the servants their presents & Fanny was simply enchanted with hers! & then off to Church. I love Xmas

morning service & the singing & everything was delightful – but oh the sermon! It really was worse than I could have imagined – and when one thinks too how easy it would be to preach Xmas day – the whole world is before one – instead of which he went meandering on for 25 minutes on doctrine! Then came lunch – turkey & plum pudding & burning brandy etc. & in the afternoon we all went out to pace up & down – Leo had quite cheered up & walked at a furious pace round & round – while we all in turns raced him with the dogs & the children flying along – it really was great fun. Father came down to lunch but wouldn't go out but sat & watched from the drawing room window. We came in & warmed up at last. M & Aunt Alice went to evening service. Leo & I went a tour round the house to watch the different stoves! He is of course quite mad on the subject! In the afternoon we went out to play to the servants & actually remembered the Handel in D! It was so nice feeling we were 3 together again & I think they all, Willis etc. liked it too. Altogether this has been such a happy Xmas – incomparably more so than the last two at any rate. It is such joy our all being here & Aunt Alice has been delightful this time. I believe it was the children – in anyway a pleasure having them – but 10 times more so if they have been the cause.

Monday 26th December

Another brilliant day ...Mr Hooley came & saw Leo – he said his whiska was too long & he had better have it cut – Leo remarked that that it was not supposed to be any use was it? Mr Hooley answered quite quietly – It prevents your food from going up your nose – that's all!! Leo was hugely pleased because Louisa the new parlour maid had [mis]taken Mr Hooley for him! Suddenly in walked Florence & Ethel Combe & were so amusing ... they said the [Cobham Park] lake was in perfect skating order & would I come. Of course I was overjoyed & started off the minute after lunch with Adele & the two children.

'Mr Hooley' was the local GP who lived in 'Broxmore' which stood on the site of Oakdene Parade at the end of the High Street. The afternoon was spent skating at Cobham Park leading Susan to write in her diary, 'the Coombes (sic) are really dears – they look after everyone so well.' More visitors arrived at Pyports in the evening for dinner and yet more music.

Equestrian Pursuits

The Surrey countryside provided the Lushingtons, who had a love of horses, with the opportunity to break away from the restrictive formality of riding in London's Rotten Row. On one occasion Susan wrote that she was trying to decide whether or not to ride, 'but I finally decided not to – tho' I felt my dear country rides are flying past – & I shall soon find myself cantering up & down the row [Rotten Row, London] ad infinitum.'[140] The Pyports meadow also offered a place in which Susan could train her horses:

> I got on my habit – jumped on my dear little Hedjay – & rode out into the field – where Willis had put up two poles – one about 2ft 9 – the other 3ft 3in – with enough space in between to get the pace up for the higher one. She jumped only once – & then did it quite beautifully ... I was just going in when I found all the servants longing to see me- so finally I had an audience of Louise, Florentine, Jessie, Katy, Maria & Mrs Woodward – who asked me to promise not to fall off! [141]

At Cobham Susan and her father tried to ride most days, often setting out at 7.30am and returning for breakfast. Their rides took them over the open commons and fields around Downside, Hatchford and Bookham or through the woods to Oxshott and Esher. Another favourite destination was Ripley where they enjoyed cantering over the village green and then calling in to see their friends the Onslows at Dunsborough Park. At this time St George's Hill was still open countryside and was another area for the Lushingtons to ride, sometimes calling in to see their friends the Egertons who had a house there. However the land here would not remain open for much longer.

The freedom to ride in the countryside around Cobham was not to last. In 1882 Vernon Lushington, after riding round St George's Hill to Weybridge and then back along the river to

Walton Bridge, wrote to his wife, 'I noticed that some sites are to be had on the south side of St. George's Hill, fronting the road to Walton Station – a beautiful position, were we seeking such.'[142] In the same year, after a long day at Kingston Court, Vernon rode home through 'Esher Woods'. He later wrote to his wife how this would be the last time because 'the Queen [who owned the Claremont estate] has ordered locks on all the gates, Her Majesty is shutting up woods which have been a pleasure to all the people round about for years & years. I can speak to 30 years & more. Sandy Lane [Cobham], I believe will remain open.'[143]

Occasionally the Lushingtons travelled further afield such as when they rode out to the Sheepleas at Horsley, on to Ranmore and then along to Newlands Corner before coming down into Guildford where they left the horses and returned by train. The next day they returned to Guildford to pick up the horses and ride on to Farnham over the Hog's Back. 'Such a glorious day & everything looked so beautiful. The view on both sides of you is magnificent.'[144] The horses were then left at Farnham while they again returned to Cobham by train. The following day they made the journey back to Farnham to pick up the horses and rode back 'all through the valley – & passed such pretty little villages – Seale, Puttenham, Compton etc. The old red-gabled cottages with the vines growing up them – looked lovely in the afternoon sun – & we got several good gallops along the various village greens and commons.' The horses were again left at Guildford and the return home was made by train to Effingham from where they were collected and driven back to Pyports giving a lift to 'a poor woman & her little girl in the rain' to Downside. 'The woman told me she had lived on 6/- [30p] per week!'[145]

The Hunt

Hunting was Susan's great passion and the 1892 Christmas hunt has already been mentioned. The Lushingtons' neighbour was Thomas Henry Bennett, Master of the Surrey Union Hunt, who kept a pack of hounds at Cobham Court. Earlier in 1892 Susan recorded in her diary how she had taken some visitors to Cobham Court to see the hounds being exercised. They talked with the huntsman and chief whip. The regular season began the following week and Susan noted with regret that she would have left Cobham by then.[146] Sadly, some years later, Bennett was seized with 'violent insanity' and was confined to the Holloway Asylum.[147]

In 1889 Susan recorded in her diary how she was invited to attend a local meet:

> [After breakfast] the gong sounded to say that Mr Bennett the huntsmen & the hounds were waiting for me. I jumped on Hedjay with all speed – & found them at the bottom of the field – I felt so proud riding along by the side of the Master – & he was so nice too – only I longed for a scarlet coat & black velvet jockey cap! We talked on and off about a good many things – he is so nice & gentle & quiet. He showed me a new way to ride to Epsom which makes it much shorter. It was rather deep & muddy but in the summer it would be very nice. The meet was in a very uninteresting place – a narrow lane – & there weren't any specially exciting people out ... I discovered Miss Watters ... who I rode with some way – but I didn't much like her. Then I struck across the fields, & had some splendid galops (sic) – falling in with heaps of other riders – but alas I had to leave them – & ride solitarily home.[148]

The following week Susan rode with Florence, Evelyn, Ethel and Kenneth Combe to meet the hunt on Bookham Common:

> We watched the riders scamper in all directions- however when we came to 100£ bridge [Hundred Pound Bridge is at the end of Bookham Common Road] – there we came in for them all – & the huntsmen & dogs ran past us. Then while they were drawing the cover on the other side we all watched ... then we had the most glorious gallop right along by Mr Coombe's (sic) farm with all the others & then they went through the gate up the hill – but 4 men – wanting to show off – tried to make their horses jump the brook – when they were all gone I made Hedjay jump it 4 times – she did

it beautifully – better than all – Then all of a sudden they scented & everyone came galloping past us.[149]

In December Susan rode to Oxshott to meet the hunt.

Mr Bennett overtook me & I rode with him up to the station – where the hounds were assembled – There I saw all the Coombes (sic) – Florence & Evelyn driving & Ethel & Kenneth riding. I joined Ethel & rode with her the whole of the time. She was quite nice – but curiously uninteresting. We went through Prince's Coverts – Then galloped away over Ashtead Common – & along the Leatherhead Road. After waiting about some time at the station Ethel & I rode home.[150]

Two earlier hunt meets are recorded in Susan's diary in 1893. The first was on 18 November when Susan:

...rode through the wood to Claygate – to the meet at Ruxley Park. It was blinding wind & rain – & they didn't start off for some time – & then spent the first hour going in & out & round & round those unending Prince's Coverts where the mud is nearly up to your horses knees. When all of sudden they got the scent & off we went. We scrambled up & down the most odious places (Fairy & I nearly came to grief over one place – a sort of deep ditch – which she didn't see & went bang into!) but at last got out of the wood – & on towards Leatherhead. It really was a grand gallop ... Fairy went simply to perfection going like the wind & passing everybody ... I came up with the hounds in front of almost everyone – but they had lost the scent – and we only pottered round Ashtead Common after that – till they went off to Epsom – & I thought I had better be going home.[151]

A few days later the hunt was closer to Cobham:

... away I rode to the meet ... there were all the Combes etc. We rode off, round Silvermere – & down into the Hatchford

Woods. It was rather dull going up and down them and Fairy would get so excited amongst the trees. Then we came back along Plough Lane & turned into Cobham Park – where we waited about for a long time – while the huntsman dismounted & took the hounds all in the water-land, down by the river. I had no idea it was so pretty. It was perfectly lovely looking down on the river & the low lying fields. I waited about for a long time & then as it was past one I thought I might as well come home – which is what I did but while I was taking off my hat I saw out of my window, the fox running across the field followed with loud shots by 5 little boys with big sticks (one of whom beat it! so it said) of course then came the riders & the hounds all in full swing. We all ran out to the bottom of the field – to see them gallop across the Leg Of Mutton Field – & they killed just at the bottom of it – oh dear – how disappointing. I had come in just 10 minutes too soon. It really was too, too exasperating – when you think it was my last hunt.[152]

When unable to ride the Lushingtons enjoyed walking in the countryside around Cobham. On an August day in 1893 Susan, with her father and her sister Margaret, travelled by carriage to Pyrford to visit Jane Lushington's grave. Susan wrote:

... we all drove off to Pyrford – It looked more lovely than I have ever seen it. We sent the carriage back & walked home. It is really the most perfect walk the whole way – & it was such joy being us three all alone – We were silent nearly altogether – which I think is the best way to walk. The sunset coming home through Mr Deacon's fields was divine.[153]

Other Pleasures

Making Music

Music was the one pastime at which all the Lushington family excelled. Jane, and later, Susan, were members of the Bach Choir. The Lushington girls often took part in musical events in the homes of their London friends as well as playing in the South Hampstead Orchestra. Jane Lushington's piano playing charmed Charles Darwin and Vernon took an active part in the promotion of the Tonic Sol Fa movement. Kitty Lushington played the cello, Margaret played the viola and Susan's instrument was the violin. They were much in demand for musical evenings and soirees held in the London homes of their many friends. In 1882 they were introduced to the composer Hubert Parry who took an instant liking to the three girls who became close lifelong friends of his young daughters, Gwen and Dolly. Parry often asked the Lushington girls to play through his new compositions and even composed especially for them. Parry asked the three sisters to give lessons to his daughters and in December 1883 Susan recorded in her diary that her sister Kitty had also given Holman Hunt's daughter Gladys her first lesson.

Music making continued at Cobham and various friends came to play with the Lushington girls. In December 1889 Florence Combe arrived at Pyports, 'with her violin & we played Haydn Quartets. She has only learnt 2 years ... she is so nice in herself & we had a nice time with her. Boyce Coombe (sic) came to fetch her.'[154]

At Pyports the family converted the barn that had been used by Samuel Bradnack for his evangelistic meetings into a small concert hall. The programmes for most of the concerts, carefully prepared by hand by the girls, have survived. A concert was always a cause for great excitement and heralded a time of activity. The pieces had to be practised and the barn decorated appropriately. In 1896 a Cobham orchestra was founded under the leadership of local resident William Tavenor and practices were held in the Pyports barn. When Tavenor died the following year, Susan Lushington temporarily took up the baton to conduct.

It was one of the barn concerts that sadly brought about the demise of Jane Lushington. On the 15 June 1884, their neighbour and friend wrote to his son, 'Poor Mrs V Lushington died on Wednesday. She had caught a cold at one of the "Barn" entertainments and could not shake it off.' Jane died in London but was buried in the churchyard of the little Norman church at Pyrford overlooking the meadows of the river Wey and only a short distance from the old farmhouse that had once been her home.

Following their mother's untimely death, the three Lushington girls were quickly taken under the wing of Sir Leslie Stephen's wife, Julia. The two families had long been the closest of friends and had spent a good deal of time in each other's London houses. It was Julia Stephen who, as we shall see, had a key role in finding a husband for Kitty Lushington.

Other concert venues in Cobham were the school in Cedar Road and the newly erected Village Hall in Anyards Road. After one concert at the Village Hall Susan Lushington wrote critically:

> Cobham is much too respectable to clap at all – & you felt it is all ferns & palms & opera-cloaks – & tight gloves – but I suppose that is because it is suburban – & also that their taste has been spoiled by 3rd rate acting ... Mrs Cushny looked a perfect vision – but her singing is horrid – trashy love songs, sentimentally sung. Miss Direham sung quite beautifully – but of course the idiotic Cobhamites didn't care for it one bit. Then Mr Helme recited – oh so badly – & poor little Miss Atlee sung – & Mrs Graham – & I played an obligato to Miss Edward's *Grand tu Chantes* – but it was too soft. There was also a tenor- who was fairly good. Well anyway it is over now – & I think the vicar was satisfied.[155]

Ethel Cushny was the young wealthy wife of Alexander Cushny who owned the Painshill estate. After her husband's death she agreed to marry the widowed Charles Combe of Cobham Park with the proviso that he purchased the Painshill estate from her late husband's executors. This he did and the two made their home at Painshill.

Another Concert, this time at Cobham Village Hall, proved a great success:

> ... Margaret & I, Gerald [Du Maurier] & Mr Furse went in the first detachment to say Howdedo to people & shew them into their seats. We found the Hall already nearly full! & by the end of the time there were people standing all round! In the front row were Admiral & Lady Louisa Egerton, with Blanche & Dorothy – & then the Bashfords! & the Barnes & of course endless 'Buxtons, Coombes (sic), Bennets, Legges, Lucy etc – & then to my joy Aunt Hester! who had come after all. I have so seldom ever played to her. I simply loved playing to her as I knew she would enjoy the dancing too. We began with the Mozart trio.[156]

'Mr Furse' was probably Michael Furse, later Bishop of St Albans. It was he who wrote to Diana Montgomery Massingberd in 1946 claiming that had first introduced Arthur Ponsonby to Dolly Parry fifty four years earlier.[157] His brother was Charles Wellington Furse, an artist who shared a studio with Susan's cousin Hugh Norris and who was an early influence on the work of Vanessa Bell before the advent of the Bloomsbury Group.

The Lushington girls were also in demand to play at the homes of their Cobham neighbours as well as venturing further afield to play in Byfleet and Weybridge at Penny Readings, a popular educational entertainment for the working classes.

Anyone For Tennis ... or Croquet?

At Pyports, in addition to riding, the whole family enjoyed playing both croquet and lawn tennis. When Christopher and Charles Howard were staying at Pyports in 1893, Susan recorded in her diary a croquet match, 'the Howard family versus "Pyports".'[158]

Despite Vernon Lushington's unorthodox religious views, playing croquet on a Sunday still presented a problem:

> We had a great discussion as to whether croquet should be allowed on the Sabbath. The rule is against [it] in this house – but Father was kind and made an exception on condition there were no signs when the Hittites & Hivites [Vernon Lushington's name for the Lushingtons of Brackenhurst] were to bear down upon us after Church. Unfortunately we didn't begin to play early enough – for we were just at the exciting crisis in the game by the time they were to be expected. However, one of us watched the gate – while the others played which really considerably enhanced the excitement – Charley & I were partners, against Christopher & Hugo – and we had been a long way behind – but we plucked up our heart just at the end – & flattered ourselves we were going to win when the signal came – & the balls had all to be chased away! On the appearance of Uncle Edward, A[un]t Mary, Stephen & Guy.[159]

Lawn tennis was a comparatively new sport which had been developed in the 1870s. A tennis court was laid out on the lawn at Pyports. Sometimes the Lushingtons played tennis at the homes of their Cobham friends. In an undated letter, an excited Susan tells of them enjoying tennis with their young friend Emmie a' Court as well as helping with the Downside School Sports and other activities:

> It is such fun playing tennis with her because she plays just about as well as us and you know we have marked out the courts with tape and hairpins (and so tightly and closely hair pinned so that you can't trip up) so we have five sets with her, her and Peg against me and Kitty. On Thursday we all went to the Deacon's school-feast, how I love it and Mrs Deacon! It was such fun swinging the children and arranging races for them, seeing which comes in first and then procuring those prizes. The Coombes (sic) were there ... Ethel and

Evelyn are going to Darmstadt into an English Family where they will learn German with a few other children, and Mr Holmes is to write and find them the best violin master! On Friday, as you know it was Kit's birthday and we went for a lovely picnic in Pyrford Woods. Some of us went in the carriage and some in the new cart, which has just come home, and is lovely, and Molly [the horse]! Emmie driving and the stable boy behind. Molly crossed the high lock bridges beautifully, and finally when we went home, they went home by Brackenhurst, and we by the Deacons, besides yesterday Emmie and Kitty went for a drive by themselves and the stable boy and tomorrow me and Peg are going, only we are going to have Willis behind. We showed Maria all over Pyrford, which she had never seen before.[160]

A Broken Engagement and Two Weddings

The two eldest Lushington sisters, Kitty and Margaret, were both married at St. Andrew's church, Cobham. Kitty had earlier been engaged for a short period to Charles Howard, the eldest son of George and Rosalind Howard, The Earl and Countess of Carlisle. It was at Pyports that, in January 1887, Kitty became engaged to Charles amidst great excitement in both families. Vernon Lushington wrote to the Howards:

> My dear Kitty brought last night the momentous news that Charlie had asked her to be his Wife. To her it came as a great surprise: to me it was a total surprise, – as sudden as the stroke of a sword.

However Lushington also expressed a note of caution concerning the young age of Charles Howard [both he and Kitty were just turned twenty]:

> Of course, I have felt a dash of difficulty in Charlie's age. Yet as you know so very well, I refuse now to court this anxiety, & will hope they may have a happy & profitable courtship, even if a little long one.[161]

Sadly Lushington's concern was to prove justified and, during a weekend visit by Charles to Pyports in April 1887, the couple broke off their engagement. It is not clear what reason was given but correspondence in the archives of Castle Howard seems to reveal that Kitty was just not ready for marriage. Susan was devastated by this event and confided in her diary, 'Life is almost unbearable any longer.' Vernon Lushington wrote to Rosalind Howard, 'Kitty's engagement we must now all admit was too precipitate. She meant right, dear child, but it was precipitate, & I deeply regret that I consented to it.'[162]

A few years later Kitty became engaged to Leopold Maxse, a young journalist and political writer the son of Admiral Maxse of nearby Dunley Hill, Effingham. Leo was something of a hypochondriac who seemed always to be suffering from chronic migraines. Kitty and Leo were brought together by the inveterate match-maker Julia Stephen who had advised the elderly G.F. Watts to waste no time in marrying Mary Fraser Tytler and had encouraged W.J. Stillman in his courtship of the beautiful model and artist Marie Spartali.

Kitty and Leo became engaged at Talland House, the Stephen family's holiday home in Cornwall which was later used by Virginia Woolf as the setting for '*To The Lighthouse*'. The couple were married in Cobham in 1890. It was the event of the year and local people had seen nothing like it since the wedding of Matthew Arnold's daughter there some years earlier. Susan Lushington wrote to her friend Hugo Montgomery about the wedding preparations. A servants' dance was held in the Pyports barn at which Susan and Margaret both performed:

> We had such fun. They had made it all look so pretty with wreaths & things & everyone was of course dressed in their best. You should have seen Emma in red silk, black lace, and diamonds! Talking a great deal, in the wildest English to everybody. Her French friend, Eugenie, was a perfect vision, in pale pink. Then there was Robert [the Lushingtons' coachman] who dances so well – Lee – Levitt, Arthur etc. We were only there from 9 till 10.30 – but they kept it up afterwards till 4AM! The musician was a funny little man, with two wooden legs, who sat on the end of the piano & fiddled.[163]

The wedding presents were displayed at Pyports for visitors to see. The Cobham tradesmen presented the young couple with a silver salt cellar together with a neatly printed card bearing all their names. The people of Downside gave a sugar basin and Mrs Matthew Arnold presented a copy of her late husband's poems. Guests at the wedding included Holman Hunt and his family and Richard and Etty Litchfield. Of course, the matriarchal matchmaker Julia Stephen attended the event together with the children from her first marriage – Stella, George and Gerald Duckworth. Julia's husband, Leslie Stephen, was absent, probably due to ill health. Another guest was Margaret Llewellyn Davies, Secretary of the Co-operative Women's Guild and aunt of the Llewellyn Davies boys who were the inspiration for J.M. Barrie's *Peter Pan*.

Kitty and Leo's wedding was marred by an unfortunate accident caused by the driver of the horse drawn omnibus which the Maxse family had hired from Dorking who, due to an excess of alcohol, lost control of the vehicle on the return journey. The carriage overturned at Downside, spilling the family and servants out onto the road. Fortunately only minor injuries were sustained. The Cobham Parish Magazine commented, 'The bride will be much missed by the poor, to whom she was a good friend. In connection with the wedding the Band of Hope were entertained at tea at Pyports on Friday evening, and on Tuesday the old people of the village were also entertained.'[164]

Three years after Kitty married Leo, her old suitor Charles Howard, returned to Pyports for a few days. Leo was also at Pyports at this time and Susan recorded how, at dinner, 'tho Margaret placed herself between Leo and Charley – and they had a lot of talk – one could see very plainly that they didn't like each other – & it was an evident effort on both sides.' However, within a matter of a few days, the two made their peace and Susan wrote,

> My heart leapt up when I looked out of my window & saw him [Leo] & Charley walking arm in arm round the garden smoking, talking over Clitheroe & the Review [The National Review – a newspaper of which Leo was the editor] – I think really it has been enormously more successful at the end than one could have hoped from the beginning. I love Leo – but alas – I feel I cannot ever get within two miles of him – I don't in the least know why.[165]

In 1894 Margaret Lushington became engaged to Stephen Massingberd of Gunby Hall in Lincolnshire. The Massingberds were an old Lincolnshire family and were related to the Wedgwood and Darwin families. Stephen's mother, Emily Caroline Massingberd, was a well-known campaigner for women's rights and a staunch teetotaller. The Massingberds' London home was at 42, Kensington Square, just a few doors from the Lushingtons' London residence. Both Stephen and his sister Diana were old friends of the family and had taken part in some of the concerts which the Lushingtons produced at Cobham Village Hall.

Margaret and Stephen were married at Cobham in 1895. The Cobham Parish Magazine reported that, 'a special train brought upwards of one hundred guests from London' for the wedding at St Andrew's church. Guest organist was the bridegroom's cousin, the young Ralph Vaughan Williams. Once again the people of Cobham turned out in force for the wedding. Flags were hung near the church and the main path from Pyports to the church was covered in crimson cloth. Family friend Arthur Munby who attended the wedding later wrote to Vernon:

> In the church, I was placed by the verger close to the bridesmaids, and just behind you and the bride and bridegroom. Thus I was in the best possible position for seeing everything, and for thinking it all over, undisturbed by the rustling of the large congregation behind. I had you, and the bride, and Kitty and Susan, in full view.

After a honeymoon spent at the home of Charles Darwin's widow in Cambridge, Margaret and Stephen settled in Lincolnshire and eventually took over Gunby Hall in 1898. The couple did much to beautify the old house and its grounds, which are now the property of the National Trust. A fine portrait of Margaret by Arthur Hughes can still be seen at Gunby.

'My Life For Others'

Vernon Lushington had inherited his family's rich spirit of reform, social concern and philanthropy. Those interests were encouraged and developed when, as a Cambridge undergraduate, he took up first the Christian Socialism of Charles Kingsley and then the Positivism of Auguste Comte. It was the latter that led him to write to his wife on the eve of their wedding, 'Don't suffer me to make an idol of home-comfort, or professional eminence, or even of yourself, my precious one! Of me too it is required, as it is required of every one that I should give my Life for others.'[166] The altruism of Comte's 'Religion of Humanity' spilled over into Cobham where Lushington and his family took an active interest both in the needs of their less well-off neighbours and in local enterprises such as that of their neighbour Miss Blunt at Church Stile House who had created a home for young women in need of shelter where they were provided with some basic training in domestic skills.

Toynbee Hall and the London Children

Whilst in Cobham the needs of people in London were not forgotten and once a year they participated in a scheme to provide children from deprived areas of the city with a country holiday. 'The Children's Country Holiday Fund' was created in 1884 by the Rev. Samuel and Mrs. Henrietta Barnett, the founders of the Toynbee Hall Settlement in London's East End. The Barnett's radical vision, named after Arnold Toynbee who had died two years earlier, was to create a place for future leaders to live and work as volunteers in London's East End, bringing them face-to-face with poverty and giving them the opportunity to develop practical solutions that they could then take with them into political and national life.

The Lushingtons were keen supporters of Toynbee Hall. Susan Lushington sang at concerts in Samuel Barnett's church of

St Jude's which adjoined Toynbee Hall and fresh flowers were occasionally sent there from the Pyports garden. Barnett, who was said to have 'had the Toryism knocked out of him in America', served as a curate to the Rev. the Hon W.H. Freemantle [later Dean of Ripon]) who married a cousin of the Lushington girls on their mother's side.

The Holiday Fund provided London children with holidays in the fresh air. Local Committees were set up to fundraise and organise the holiday and children were placed for two weeks with people who had cottages or other properties in the countryside and villages surrounding the city. In July 1886 Susan Lushington wrote in her diary that she had been to Ockham 'to see about the Children's Holiday Fund, as we are going to have some children down. Kitty & M[argaret] went to Downside for the same purpose.'[167]

The following year Vernon Lushington wrote to his old friend William Bell Scott:

> My girls are all well. Just now they are busy with 114 London children under their wing – that is boarded out for a fortnight with the cottagers in the Village & round about. The scheme works well & does a great deal of good not only to the children, but to the cottagers & all concerned. The children on the whole behave extremely well – Sometimes however it is necessary to scold them, & this task falls to Kitty or Margaret. Both are effective; but Margaret I believe on such occasions – withering, terrible! To hearten up the foster mothers & other humble neighbours, the girls are giving a series of Concerts in the Barn. Very good music they give & they have crowded audiences, mothers & babies, stout men from their work, old people & infirm- Last night was their third concert. At the second they had a good friend to help, our Irish landlord Hugh Montgomery, who sang them 'Tom Bowling' & 'Come Lasses & Lads' in fine style – Tears have been seen to flow in that Barn.[168]

There was always great excitement when the children arrived at Cobham by train:

> The train was ½ an hour late, owing to the holiday makers, but it was most refreshing to see all the children waving their hands as the train came up. We made them all sit down while we tied on the labels, & then after putting the parcels into the waggonette we walked off home. We had any amount of games etcetera in the field, & also tea, & then came the fearful business of separating those children who Margaret & I were to take to Downside & Bookham.[169]

The waggonette for the children's parcels belonged John Reading of Church Gate House who was the local 'fly proprietor' – the equivalent of a today's taxi driver. The children did not always arrive together and the Lushingtons were sometimes faced with finding more homes both for the late comers and the ladies who escorted them. Resources were stretched In August 1887 when additional accommodation had to be found for Ada de Morgan who had brought down two children as well as Mrs Griffiths who was the wife of the Co-operative Secretary and her four children. In July 1890 there were:

> only 52 instead of 93 [children] so it was much easier ... We managed very skilfully to pack them all in the omnibus & a little pony cart so that there was only Margaret & me & the bigger boys walking. We divided up at Downside. Kitty went on to Bookham in the omnibus – Margaret went home & took some boys up to the Tartar Hill & I drove the little pony cart & 8 children to Chatley. We all got home about the same time – 8.30 PM – pretty well done. Oh the joy of a quiet evening & to bed.[170]

Vernon's comments to Bell Scott regarding Margaret's handling of the children are confirmed in a letter from her to Kitty in 1886:

> I'm afraid I rather wish the race of children could be swept off the face of the earth. When we reached Downside this

> afternoon we were met by Mrs West, saying she couldn't think of taking any more children. Maurice Davies has been so frightfully naughty & so has Holden that the poor woman was nearly ill. We offered to take them away but she said that as she has borne with them for a week she would try to for this week. So then after placing the other children (only 22 came by the bye so we had to rearrange) Sue & I set off for Crab & Holden & gave it them very very hot, so I trust they'll behave better in future. Dear little Mrs Stratford was delighted with her two wee boys & I think she'll be doubly good to them because of our first little row. Dora was found weeping at the gate because she said a little girl told her she had asked for meat 4 times a day! So I'm glad it's coming home to her. [171]

As the children were dispersed around Cobham, Downside and Bookham, Pyports became the focus for their activities. In addition to musical entertainments and a conjuring show from William Bethel, other activities and games were provided such as cricket in the Pyports meadow. There were firm rules about where the children could go. They were not allowed into the garden and the river was strictly out of bounds. Despite that some of the boys found their way there only to return to Pyports for a 'real scolding'. In 1888 a hundred children sat down to tea in the barn.

The Lushington girls also worked together with their friend Lucy Martineau of Weybridge who found homes for some children in her part of Surrey. At Cobham they were sometimes helped by Miss Lorenzo Rodd, a member of the Positivist group, who came to stay at Pyports. After the children returned to London it was left to Susan and Miss Rodd to visit all the homes where the children had stayed and pay the hosts.

Occasionally some of the children had to be taken back to London early. Margaret Lushington wrote to her sister Kitty about one such time. The letter reveals the very real concern that the Lushingtons had for the London families as when Margaret suggests that they should spend more time in the Whitechapel area when they were in London.

> Little Kate, Julia & I started then directly we went all the way to Waterloo. Then walked to Westminster Bridge where we took a train to St Mary's, Whitechapel from where we walked to her home. Poor wee thing, she was quiet all the way till we came to their house when she burst into pitiful sobs. The sister opened the door & it was so pathetic to see the mother (quite young & so pretty, married at 13) trying to soothe Kate & check her own sobbing – poor, poor creatures. Kit we must try & live a little more with these people when we come to town. The streets were so bitterly interesting you felt you could never leave them. The Smiths house though miserably poor was spic & span clean.[172]

There was always sadness tinged with relief when the children returned to London and Margaret Lushington picked flowers so that little bunches could be given to each child to take home.

Endings

After Kitty and Margaret married and moved away from Cobham, Vernon and Susan Lushington found that Pyports was too large for their requirements and, in any event, the lease was coming to an end. So it was that in 1903 they said goodbye to Cobham, where they were greatly missed, and left to set up home in the Hampshire village of Kingsley near Bordon. Here they settled in the house that had formerly belonged to Vernon's two sisters Frances and Alice who died in 1900 and 1903 respectively.

Margaret Massingberd and her husband Stephen lived at Gunby Hall, Lincolnshire where they both encouraged, and participated in, local musical events. They helped establish a music festival in which they were supported by the young Ralph Vaughan Williams who stayed at Gunby Hall and found inspiration from the surrounding countryside for compositions such as *In The Fen Country*. Sadly, Margaret died suddenly and unexpectedly in 1906 after suffering from a burst appendix.

Vernon Lushington, who increasingly suffered from rheumatism, made regular visits to Bath during the closing years of his life in the hope of finding some measure of relief. He died peacefully in his sleep in 1912 having outlived many of his better known old friends such as Rossetti whose funeral he attended in 1882; Holman Hunt at whose funeral in 1910 he had to decline being a pallbearer because of his own frailty, and in 1896 William Morris whom he called 'the friend of my youth'.

After her marriage to Leopold Maxse, Kitty became established as one of London's leading hostesses, holding parties for friends and associates of her husband who had acquired a reputation for himself in the world of journalism and newspapers. After the death of Sir Leslie Stephen, Kitty Lushington assumed maternal care for the Stephen children including Virginia and Vanessa who, with other friends, later formed the Bloomsbury Group. Initially Kitty was enthusiastic about Virginia and her brother Adrian setting up 'some sort of nice interesting life for themselves together'.[173] However as the group developed and were joined by friends whose life styles did not accord with Edwardian proprieties, Kitty distanced herself and was later 'cut' by Virginia when they both attended the funeral of an old mutual friend. Despite this, Virginia remained fascinated by Kitty and her life style and used her as the model for 'Mrs Dalloway' – the brilliant London hostess. When Kitty died in somewhat mysterious circumstances after falling over a bannister at their London house in 1922, Virginia mischievously hinted that it might have been suicide although there is no evidence to support that idea.

Susan Lushington never married but, at Kingsley, she lived a full and busy life to the end. She was very active in local affairs and supported the village school where she had a way of walking in, 'interrupting lessons to ask for her dancing eight, who were highly delighted to be whisked away to dance at a Garden Party or Wedding.'[174] In 1943 she was awarded the MBE for her services to music. In the 1940s when there was a re-awakening of interest in Victorian art and the Pre-Raphaelites she was able to relate stories and anecdotes not only from her own past but also those she had heard from her father. During the Second World War she turned over many of the rooms in the old school building to foreign evacuees and military officers, and her entertainment of soldiers from the neighbouring barracks was so lavish that her friends protested. After Dunkirk a sign appeared on the front door, 'Returned Heroes – please walk in and briefly phone your families – it's FREE.' [175]

In the early 1940s Susan invited a young journalist William Gaunt to stay in one of the cottages at Kingsley. Gaunt went on to write one of the first major reviews of the Pre-Raphaelite movement drawing from letters and papers in Susan's possession as well as from her own personal recollections. His book *The Pre-Raphaelite Tragedy*, published in 1942, launched his career as an art historian.

Susan is remembered in her closing years by Gabrielle Griswold who stayed with her for a short period during the spring of 1952:

> No sooner had I moved in than Susan and I settled into a routine – if anything could be called routine where Susan

> was concerned. One of her eccentricities was her timetable which was not that of ordinary mortals. She stayed up late at night and rose late in the morning. I never learned what her bedtimes were or what all she did in the wee hours of the night, flitting about the house ... And while all the horde of various other inmates slept snug and silent in their beds, she and the house entered into a mystic communion of their own. Then she danced with the dogs, padded about attending to correspondence or to flowers, nipping the dead blooms, looked at her pictures, read and reminisced over her girlhood diaries.[176]

Susan died in 1953 and was buried in Kingsley churchyard. Her obituary in *The Journal of the English Folk Dance & Song Society* states, 'Susan Lushington was a woman of quite exceptional gifts, which she employed mainly in the cause of music ... Her triumph was to make music live, to show that it was not a thing apart, for the specialist only, but for the enjoyment of "as many as will" ... she leaves a gap which will not be filled.'[177] For a while after Susan's death Ockham Schools at Kingsley were left empty and open to vandalism. Precious letters and paintings were at risk and some were lost. Susan's death brought to an end of a remarkable family whose lives spanned over 150 years linking the Clapham Sect of the early nineteenth century to the Bloomsbury Group of the early twentieth century.

The fortunate survival and re-discovery of the Lushington family archive means that the family's unique contribution to the intellectual, legal, spiritual and social development of this country can now be properly assessed. In particular Vernon Lushington's journey from Christian Socialism to the Positivism of Auguste Comte; his contributions to the intellectual and cultural life of the second half of the nineteenth century and the way in which his life is intertwined with many of the eminent Victorians whom he counted as his friends, is a story that needs to be told – but that's for another book!

1 Vernon Lushington to Susan Lushington, 25 July 1905. SHC 7854/4/2/319.
2 *Thomas Lushington (1590-1661)*, New Oxford Dictionary of National Biography.
3 For more on Thomas Lushington, see H.J. McLachlan, *Socinianism in Seventeenth-Century England* (OUP, 1951).
4 For more on the Lushingtons and Tennysons see John O. Waller, *A Circle of Friends: The Tennysons and the Lushingtons of Park House* (Ohio State Press, 1986).
5 Sir Stephen had been created a baronet in 1791 and, on his death, the title passed to his eldest son Henry. Sir Stephen's wife was Hester (d. 1830), daughter of John Boldero of Aspenden Hall, Hertfordshire.
6 A full account of Lushington's representation of the Queen is in S.M. Waddams, *Law, Politics and the Church of England. The Career of Stephen Lushington 1782-1783* (CUP 1992).
7 Stephen Lushington to Henry Brougham, 9 August 1821. *The Creevey Papers: A selection from the Correspondence and Diaries of the late Thomas Creevey, M.P.* (Cambridge University Press, 1903), Vol. 2, p. 22.
8 *The Morning Post*, 10 August 1821, reported "Married, on Wednesday, at Hampstead Church, Dr. Lushington, the distinguished Counsel of her late MAJESTY, to Miss CARR, daughter of THOMAS W.CARR, Esq. Solicitor to the Excise. Dr. Lushington, it is supposed, will proceed almost immediately to Brunswick, for the purposes relating to the removal of her MAJESTY'S remains to that place for internment.
9 For more on this event see Christopher Hibbert, *George IV. Regent and King*, (Allen Lane, 1973).
10 Lady Seymour (ed.) *The "Pope" of Holland House: Selections from the correspondence of John Wishaw and his friends, 1813-40* (T.F. Unwin, 1906), p. 240.
11 Joanna Baillie to Lady Dacre, 15 August 1821.
12 Maria Edgeworth to Harriet Butler, 16 March 1831. Christina Colvin ed., *Maria Edgeworth, Letters From England 1813-1844*, (Oxford, Clarendon Press, 1971).
13 Charles a' Court Repington, *Vestiga. Reminiscences of Peace and War* (1919).
14 Vernon Lushington to H.G. Seeley, 29 January 1865.
15 Elizabeth Gaskell to Vernon Lushington, 11 January 1865.
15a David Taylor, *An Estate For All Seasons. A History of Cobham Park, Surrey and its Owners and Occupiers.* (Phillimore & Co. Ltd. 2006), p.65.
16 Jane to Vernon, 23 July 1877. SHC 7854/3/6/14/17.
17 Jane to Vernon, 3 August 1877. SHC 7854/3/6/14/26.
18 Vernon to Jane, 2 August 1877. SHC 7854/3/5/14/25.
19 Vernon to Jane, 3 August 1877. SHC 7854/3/5/14/26.
20 Jane to Vernon, 4 August 1877. SHC 7854/3/6/14/27.

21 Jane to Vernon, 18 September 1877. SHC 7854/3/6/14/29.
22 Jane to Vernon, 11 October 1877. SHC 7854/3/6/14/33.
23 Jane to Vernon, 22 October 1877. SHC 7854/3/6/14/37.
24 SHC K44/11/7.
25 Jane to Vernon, 11 December 1879. SHC 7854/3/6/16/45.
26 Jane to Vernon, 11 December 1879. SHC 7854/3/6/16/45.
27 Jane to Vernon, 15 October 1878. SHC 7854/3/6/15/28.
28 Jane to Vernon, 5 September 1879. SHC 7854/5/6/16/29.
29 Jane to Vernon, 15 October 1878. SHC 7854/3/6/28.
30 Jane to Vernon, July 1878. SHC 7854/3/6/15/18.
31 Susan Lushington's Diary. 23 July 1889. SHC 7854/4/1/1/7.
32 Vernon to Jane, [nd]. SHC 7854/3/5/4/23.
33 Susan Lushington's Diary. 19 May 1891. SHC 7854/4/1/1/9.
34 Susan Lushington's Diary. 3 September 1893. SHC7854/4/1/1/11.
35 Susan Lushington's Diary. 8 August 1893. SHC 7854/4/1/1/11.
36 Susan Lushington's Diary. 13 August 1893. SHC 7854/4/1/1/11.
37 Margaret Lushington to Jane Lushington, 13 August 1878. SHC 7854/3/14/1.
38 William Robinson to Susan Lushington, 17 October 1932. SHC 7854/4/3/13.
39 Vernon to Jane, 5 November 1878. SHC 7854/3/5/15/4.
40 Jane to Vernon, 7 September 1878. SHC 7854/3/6/16/27.
41 Jane to Vernon, 4 September 1879. SHC 7854/3/6/16/29.
42 Vernon to Jane, 25 March 1880. SHC 7854/3/5/17/2.
43 Vernon to Susan, 4 October 1895. SHC 7854/4/2/11.
44 Margaret Lushington to Kitty Lushington, October 1886. SHC 7854/4/3.
45 Susan Lushington's Diary. 20 August 1893. SHC 7854/4/1/1/11.
46 Margaret Lushington to Kitty Lushington, [nd] SHC 7854/5/3/49.
47 Jane to Vernon, 8 September 1878. SHC 7854/3/6/28.
48 Jane to Vernon, 22 November 1878. SHC 7854/3/6/15/36.
49 Jane to Vernon, 21 August 1879. SHC 7854/3/6/16/25.
50 Rowena Russell to Jane Lushington, 11 February 1879. SHC 7854/36/16/4.
51 Susan Lushington's Diary. 17 November 1892. SHC 7854/4/1/1/10.
52 Susan Lushington to Hugh Montgomery, 12 Nov 1895. SHC 7854/9/34.
53 Margaret Lushington to Kitty Lushington, [nd]. SHC 7854/4/3/14.
54 Susan Lushington's Diary. 9 August 1893. SHC 7854/4/1/1/11.
55 Joanna Baillie to Henrietta Baillie. 21 August 1838. *The Letters of Joanna Baillie* Vol. 2.
56 Jane to Vernon. 21 October 1872, SHC 7854/3/5/11.
57 The National Archives. C211/46.
58 Laura Lushington to Susan Lushington, 24 March 1909. SHC 7854/4/7/9/1.
59 Susan Lushington's Diary.12 November 1886, SHC 7854/4/1/1/4.
60 Susan Lushington's Diary. 6 October 1882, SHC 7854/4/1/1/1.
61 William Holman Hunt to Vernon Lushington, 2 November 1884. Princeton University.

62 Susan Lushington's Diary. 15 December 1889. SHC 7854/4/1/1/7.

63 Vernon Lushington contributed an essay on this painting and on D.G. Rossetti's "Dante's Vision of Beatrice" to *The Oxford and Cambridge Magazine.*

64 Lushington's letters to Hughes are in the National Art Library.

65 Jane to Vernon. 14 February 1883. SHC 7854/3/6/20/6.

66 Susan Lushington's Diary. 28 April to 2 May 1885. Hughes was back at Pyports in 1886 to work on the portrait - see Susan Lushington's Diary 20 November to 22 November 1886.

67 Susan Lushington's Diary. 6 September 1883. SHC 7854/4/1/1/2.

68 William Bell Scott to Arthur J. Munby, 8 July 1884. University of Chicago Library. N 79.52.

69 Vernon Lushington to Kitty Lushington. 4 September 188. SHC 7854/5/1/118.

70 Susan Lushington's Diary. 27 November 1885. SHC 7854/4/1/1/3.

71 Susan Lushington's Diary. 25 February 1893. SHC 7854/4/1/1/11.

72 Susan Lushington's Diary. 18 August 1893. SHC 7854/4/1/1/11.

73 Margaret Lushington to Kitty Lushington [nd] SHC 7854/4/3/15.

74 Julia Stephen to Vernon Lushington. 16 February 1887. SHC 7854/3/2/88.

75 Susan Lushington's Diary. 24 February 1887. SHC 7854/4/1/1/5.

76 Gwent Raveratt, *A Cambridge Childhood.*

77 Susan Lushington's Diary. 17 August 1894. SHC 7854/4/1/1/12.

78 Susan Lushington's Diary. 19 August 1894. SHC 7854/4/1/1/12.

79 Susan Lushington's Diary. 25 August 1894. SHC 7854/4/1/1/12.

80 Vernon Lushington to Kitty Lushington. [nd]. SHC 7854/5/1/119.

81 Susan Lushington's Diary. 26 to 28 November 1892. SHC/4/1/1/10.

82 Susan Lushington's Diary. 15 November 1893. SHC 7854/4/1/1/11.

83 For Munby's visit to Cobham see David C. Taylor, *Cobham Characters* (Appleton Publications, 1997).

84 Susan Lushington's Diary. 18 September 1892. SHC 7854/4/1/1/10.

85 Susan Lushington's Diary. 19 July 1894. SHC 7854/4/1/1/12.

86 Margaret Lushington's Diary. 18 July 1894. SHC 7854/6/1/2.

87 Susan Lushington's Diary. 19 July 1894. SHC 7854/4/1/1/12.

88 Susan Lushington's Diary. 5 August 1891. SHC 7854/4/1/1/9.

89 Susan Lushington's Diary. 5 August 1891. SHC 7854/4/1/1/9.

90 *Moments of Being*, Virginia Woolf, p.149.

91 Susan Lushington's Diary. 13 May 1894. SHC 7854/4/1/1/12.

91a In 1981 John Montgomery Massingberd wrote to the author, 'I in fact owe a very special debt to the Lushington family since it so happens that they were the mutual friends through whom Montgomerys and Massingberds first met.'

92 Susan Lushington's Diary. 5 August 1893. SHC 7854/4/1/1/11.

93 Susan Lushington's Diary. 9 August 1893. SHC 7854/4/1/1/11.

94 Henrietta Litchfield [Darwin's daughter] to Jane Lushington, 29 October 1877. SHC 7854/3/5/14/32.

95 Jane to Vernon. [nd] SHC 7854/4/2/692.
96 Susan Lushington Diary. 22 August 1893. SHC 7854/4/1/1/11.
97 On 6 August 1889 Susan recorded in her diary how she had visited the Casenoves "at their new house."
98 Jane to Vernon. 28 August 1883. SHC 7854/3/6/20/43.
99 Susan Lushington's Diary. 12 August 1893. SHC 7854/4/1/1/11.
100 Susan Lushington's Diary. 17 August 1889. SHC 7854/4/1/1/7.
101 Vernon Lushington to Susan Lushington. 25 September 1897. SHC 7854/4/2/33.
102 Jane to Vernon. 13 October 1879. SHC 7854/3/6/16/36. In 1939, with the threat of the Second World War, Wesley's school moved from Cobham to Rushmore House in the centre of Cranborne Chase on the borders of Wiltshire and Dorset where it has remained ever since.
103 Susan Lushington's Diary. 16 November 1891. SHC 7854/4/1/1/9.
104 Susan Lushington's Diary. 7 December 1893. SHC 7854/4/1/1/11.
105 Susan Lushington's Diary. 12 November 1891. SHC 7854/4/1/1/9.
106 Susan Lushington's Diary. 31 December 1892. SHC 7854/4/1/1/10.
107 Susan Lushington's Diary. 31 December 1892. SHC 7854/4/1/1/10.
108 Susan Lushington's Diary. 1 & 2 January 1893. SHC 7854/4/1/1/10.
109 Susan Lushington's Diary. 4 January 1893. SHC 7854/4/1/1/11.
110 Susan Lushington's Diary. 16 November 1893. SHC 7854/4/1/1/11.
111 Susan Lushington's Diary. 20 July 1893. SHC 7854/4/1/1/11.
112 Margaret Lushington to Kitty Lushington. 7 Oct [no year]. SHC 7854/4/3/17.
113 Jane to Vernon. 9 Aug 1882. SHC 7854/3/5/19/16.
114 Jane to Vernon. Aug 1882. SHC 7854/3/6/19/20.
115 Jane to Vernon. 18 November 1880. SHC 7854/3/6/17/24.
116 Matthew Arnold to Frances Arnold, 6 November 1882.
117 Margaret Lushington to Kitty Lushington. [nd] SHC 7854/5/3/8.
118 Margaret Lushington to Kitty Lushington. [nd] SHC 7854//3/45.
119 Matthew Arnold to Lucy Whitridge. 3 December 1887.
120 Susan Lushington's Diary. 30 October 1892. SHC 7854/4/1/10.
121 Susan Lushington's Diary. 25 August 1893. SHC 7854/4/1/1/11.
122 Susan Lushington's Diary. 30 August 1893. SHC 7854/4/1/1/11.
123 Susan Lushington's Diary. 2 September 1893. SHC 7854/4/1/1/11.
124 Vernon Lushington to Kitty Lushington. 27 September 1888. SHC 7854/5/1/3.
125 Margaret to Susan Lushington. October 1886. SHC 7854/5/3/7.
126 Susan Lushington's Diary. 19 April 1885. SHC 7854/4/1/1/3.
127 Susan Lushington's Diary. 19 July 1887. SHC 7854/4/1/1/5.
128 Susan Lushington's Diary. 13 October 1889. SHC 7854/4/1/1/7.
129 Susan Lushington's Diary. 20 December 1889. SHC 7854/4/1/1/7.
130 Susan Lushington Diary. 23 October 1892. SHC 7854/4/1/1/10.
131 Susan Lushington's Dairy. 20 November 1892. SHC 7854/1/1/10.

132 Susan Lushington to Kitty Lushington [nd]. SHC 7854/5/4/17/6.
133 Jane to Vernon. 21 September 1871. SHC 7854/3/6/7/35.
134 Gerard Banks became curate of Cobham in 1861, leaving after three years for Newton Abbot, Devon. He returned to Cobham as vicar in 1867 but resigned in 1884 owing to ill health. Banks reputedly had a "clear and powerful voice."
135 John Pyke Hullah was a composer and teacher of music who was opposed to the Tonic sol-fa system.
136 Jane to Vernon. 6 September 1878. SHC 7854/3/5/15/22.
137 Susan Lushington's Diary. 15 July 1885. SHC 7854/4/1/1/3.
138 Susan Lushington's Diary. 25 July 1893. SHC 7854/4/1/11.
139 Margaret Lushington to Hugh Montgomery. 26 December 1890. SHC 7854/9/36.
140 Susan Lushington's Diary. 21 November 1889. SHC 7854/7.
141 Susan Lushington's Diary. 13 December 1889. SHC 7854/7.
142 Vernon to Jane. 13 September 1882. SHC 7854/3/5/19/36.
143 Vernon to Jane. 15 September 1882. SHC 7854/3/5/19/38.
144 Susan Lushington's Diary. 10 December 1889. SHC 7854/7.
145 Susan Lushington's Diary. 11 September 1889. SHC 7854/7.
146 Susan Lushington's Diary, 23 October 1892. SHC4/1/1/10.
147 Vernon Lushington to Susan Lushington. 1 & 2 October [1897]
148 Susan Lushington's Diary. 19 November 1889. SHC 7854/1/1/7.
149 Susan Lushington's Diary. 23 November 1889. SHC 7854/1/1/7.
150 Susan Lushington's Diary. 10 December 1889. SHC 7854/1/1/7.
151 Susan Lushington's Diary. 18 November 1893. SHC 7854/1/1/11.
152 Susan Lushington's Diary. 25 November 1893. SHC 7854/1/1/11.
153 Susan Lushington's Diary. 23 August 1893. SHC 7854/1/1/11.
154 Susan Lushington's Diary. 9 December 1889. SHC 7854/1/1/7.
155 Susan Lushington's Diary. 6 November 1889. SHC 7854/1/1/7.
156 Susan Lushington's Diary. 11 December 1893. SHC 7854/1/1/10.
157 Diana Montgomery Massingberd to Susan Lushington. 6 May 1946. SHC 7854/4/11/3/52.
158 Susan Lushington's Diary. 29 July 1893. SHC 7854/4/1/11.
159 Susan Lushington's Diary. 30 July 1893. SHC 7854/4/1/11.
160 Susan Lushington to Vernon Lushington. [nd] SHC7854/3/6/19/55.
161 Castle Howard Reference J23/67.
162 Vernon Lushington to Rosalind Howard 28 April 1887. Castle Howard Reference J23/67.
163 Susan Lushington to Hugh Montgomery. 26 December 1890.
164 Cobham Parish Magazine. January 1891.
165 Susan Lushington's Diary. 31 July 1893. SHC 7854/4/4/1/11.
166 Vernon to Jane, 1865. SHC7854/3/1.
167 Susan Lushington's Diary. 22 July 1886. SHC 7854/4/1/1/4.

168 Vernon Lushington to William Bell Scott, 10 August 1887. Collection of Mark Samuels Lasner, University of Delaware Library.
169 Susan Lushington's Diary. 30 July 1887. SHC 7854/4/1/1/5.
170 Susan Lushington's Diary. 29 July 1890. SHC 7854/4/1/1/8.
171 Margaret to Kitty Lushington. 11 August 1886. SHC 7854/5/3/1.
172 Margaret to Kitty Lushington. [nd] SHC 7854/4/3/63.
173 Kitty Maxse to Susan Lushington. 1 December 1906. SHC 7854/7854/4/4/54.
174 Recollections of Winifred Barnes of Kingsley.
175 For more on Susan Lushington see Helen Penn Mirwald & Martha S. Vogeler, *A Life Devoted to Music: Susan Lushington in Kingsley*. Hampshire Field Club Archaeological Society, 1999.
176 By kind permission of Gabrielle Griswold.
177 *The Journal of the English Folk Dance & Song Society*, vol. 7, no. 2, December 1953.

Index

Lightning Source UK Ltd.
Milton Keynes UK
UKOW01f2159090616

275930UK00005B/81/P

9 781781 48403